CONTROVERSIES

The Elderly

Other Books in the Current Controversies Series

The Elderly

Sylvia Engdahl, Book Editor

GREENHAVEN PRESS
A part of Gale, Cengage Learning

Detroit • New York • San Francisco • New Haven, Conn • Waterville, Maine • London

GALE
CENGAGE Learning

Christine Nasso, *Publisher*
Elizabeth Des Chenes, *Managing Editor*

© 2011 Greenhaven Press, a part of Gale, Cengage Learning

Gale and Greenhaven Press are registered trademarks used herein under license.

For more information, contact:
Greenhaven Press
27500 Drake Rd.
Farmington Hills, MI 48331-3535
Or you can visit our Internet site at gale.cengage.com

Articles in Greenhaven Press anthologies are often edited for length to meet page requirements. In addition, original titles of these works are changed to clearly present the main thesis and to explicitly indicate the author's opinion. Every effort is made to ensure that Greenhaven Press accurately reflects the original intent of the authors. Every effort has been made to trace the owners of copyrighted material.

Cover image photos.com/Getty Images.

LIBRARY OF CONGRESS CATALOGING-IN-PUBLICATION DATA

The elderly / Sylvia Engdahl, book editor.
    p. cm. -- (Current controversies)
    Includes bibliographical references and index.
    ISBN 978-0-7377-5179-6 (hbk.) -- ISBN 978-0-7377-5180-2 (pbk.)
    1. Older people--United States--Juvenile literature. 2. Older people--Juvenile literature. I. Engdahl, Sylvia.
    HQ1064.U5E39653 2011
    305.260973--dc22
                                                                    2010043795

Printed in the United States of America
1 2 3 4 5 6 7 15 14 13 12 11

Contents

Chapter 1: How Do Negative Stereotypes Affect Americans' Perception of the Elderly?

Thomas Day

American society glorifies youth and despises old age. The media depict old people as weak, incompetent, or even comical. This has resulted in both the elderly themselves and the community regarding older people as less valuable than younger individuals. Many elderly individuals buy into the notion that they are no longer useful; thus their negative attitude toward aging becomes self-fulfilling.

Robert Butler, as told to Patrick Perry

Sounding a call to action, a renowned expert on aging examines the health, economic, and social challenges as well as the opportunities of growing older in today's society.

Jamie Hanlon

Researchers have found that children develop negative stereotypes about elderly people's cognitive ability by the age of three, although those who had been exposed to older adults were less prone to do so. This bias affects not only children's interaction with the elderly throughout their lives, but also their own self-concept when they themselves grow old.

Chapter 2: Are Elderly People Unhappy with Their Lives?

According to some researchers, older adults are happier and more optimistic than younger ones, whose lives tend to be more stressful. But other researchers believe that such findings are misleading because they compare people with the same income levels, health, and family situations, whereas a greater proportion of the elderly have low incomes, are not in good health, and live alone.

Yes: Old Age Is a Time of Decline and Loss

Nothing is more personal than an individual's choice of how to spend his or her final years, but government bureaucracy sometimes interferes. For example, an elderly gay couple who had a long-term relationship were separated when one of the partners became ill and was hospitalized; the partners were not allowed to see each other again, and authorities sold their joint possessions.

No: Elderly People Often Find Happiness

Chapter 3: Should More Medical Care Be Provided to the Elderly?

The elderly are dangerously overmedicated. Adverse drug reactions are more frequent in people over sixty-five than in younger adults and may be the cause of symptoms that are attributed to aging, especially when multiple drugs are being taken. Yet the elderly are culturally predisposed to expect medication and are apt to feel disregarded if it is not given to them.

Chapter 4: What Major Problems Are Common Among the Elderly?

Foreword

By definition, controversies are "discussions of questions in which opposing opinions clash" (Webster's Twentieth Century Dictionary Unabridged). Few would deny that controversies are a pervasive part of the human condition and exist on virtually every level of human enterprise. Controversies transpire between individuals and among groups, within nations and between nations. Controversies supply the grist necessary for progress by providing challenges and challengers to the status quo. They also create atmospheres where strife and warfare can flourish. A world without controversies would be a peaceful world; but it also would be, by and large, static and prosaic.

The Series' Purpose

The purpose of the Current Controversies series is to explore many of the social, political, and economic controversies dominating the national and international scenes today. Titles selected for inclusion in the series are highly focused and specific. For example, from the larger category of criminal justice, Current Controversies deals with specific topics such as police brutality, gun control, white collar crime, and others. The debates in Current Controversies also are presented in a useful, timeless fashion. Articles and book excerpts included in each title are selected if they contribute valuable, long-range ideas to the overall debate. And wherever possible, current information is enhanced with historical documents and other relevant materials. Thus, while individual titles are current in focus, every effort is made to ensure that they will not become quickly outdated. Books in the Current Controversies series will remain important resources for librarians, teachers, and students for many years.

In addition to keeping the titles focused and specific, great care is taken in the editorial format of each book in the series. Book introductions and chapter prefaces are offered to provide background material for readers. Chapters are organized around several key questions that are answered with diverse opinions representing all points on the political spectrum. Materials in each chapter include opinions in which authors clearly disagree as well as alternative opinions in which authors may agree on a broader issue but disagree on the possible solutions. In this way, the content of each volume in Current Controversies mirrors the mosaic of opinions encountered in society. Readers will quickly realize that there are many viable answers to these complex issues. By questioning each author's conclusions, students and casual readers can begin to develop the critical thinking skills so important to evaluating opinionated material.

Current Controversies is also ideal for controlled research. Each anthology in the series is composed of primary sources taken from a wide gamut of informational categories including periodicals, newspapers, books, U.S. and foreign government documents, and the publications of private and public organizations. Readers will find factual support for reports, debates, and research papers covering all areas of important issues. In addition, an annotated table of contents, an index, a book and periodical bibliography, and a list of organizations to contact are included in each book to expedite further research.

Perhaps more than ever before in history, people are confronted with diverse and contradictory information. During the Persian Gulf War, for example, the public was not only treated to minute-to-minute coverage of the war, it was also inundated with critiques of the coverage and countless analyses of the factors motivating U.S. involvement. Being able to sort through the plethora of opinions accompanying today's major issues, and to draw one's own conclusions, can be a complicated and frustrating struggle. It is the editors' hope that Current Controversies will help readers with this struggle.

Introduction

"The number of elderly people—'older adults,' or 'elders,' as they are increasingly referred to by advocates for their welfare—has grown significantly in the United States during the past few decades, and it is expected to grow even faster during the next few years."

The number of elderly people—"older adults," or "elders," as they are increasingly referred to by advocates for their welfare—has grown significantly in the United States during the past few decades, and it is expected to grow even faster during the next few years. According to the U.S. Administration on Aging, there were 38.9 million Americans over sixty-five years old in 2008, an increase of 4.5 million since 1998. The number of people sixty-five and older is expected to rise from 40 million in 2010 to 55 million in 2020, a 36 percent increase. Nearly one out of five Americans will then be over sixty-five, as compared to about one out of eight now.

There are two reasons why the percentage of older adults is increasing. First, the "baby boomers," the generation that began with those born shortly after World War II when the birth rate was exceptionally high, will reach sixty-five starting in 2011. Second, people are living longer than they used to. Average life expectancy has increased dramatically during the past century; however, because the increases were due mainly to a drop in the death rate of children and younger people, this has had less effect on how long older adults will live than is often claimed. It is not true that the rise in life expectancy at birth from about sixty-two years in 1935 to about seventy-eight in 2010 means the average elder will have sixteen more years of life than he or she could have expected when Social

Security was established. Nevertheless, elders do have more years remaining at age sixty-five than they did a half-century ago—an average of about four more for men and five more for women. Furthermore, those over eighty-five years old are the fastest-growing group of all.

The prospect of a lengthening life span is of course good news to most people, but to many economists, it is worrisome. They fear that having a larger proportion of people collecting retirement payments, as compared to the number of people who are working, will mean that the money for these benefits will run out. For this reason, the traditional retirement age of sixty-five is gradually being raised to sixty-seven, and some propose raising it even higher. Others argue that not all people over sixty-five are in good enough health to work, and if they are in poor health yet not old enough for Social Security they will have to receive disability payments, which come from the same "pot" of government money. Another major worry of economists and social planners is that no solution is in sight for the problem of providing long-term care for the growing number of elders who are chronically ill or suffer from dementia. Further, there are people who feel that if society devotes a large proportion of its resources to the old, it will come at the expense of the young. On the other hand, it has been pointed out that before Social Security existed, families bore the entire responsibility for supporting aging relatives, so supporting the elderly through taxes does not really cost families more.

These are serious issues that are bound to cause controversy in the coming decades. But advocates for the elderly point out that it should not be thought, as it too often is, that older adults as a group are a burden on society. On the contrary, the majority are contributors, either because they continue to work—as more and more are doing by necessity or by choice—or as volunteers. Then too, many have investment income on which they pay taxes. Only elders who are ill can be considered dependent; most retired people are in good health and do not want to be viewed as different from anybody else. Additionally, elders are far more involved in the same pursuits as younger adults—such as travel, creative arts, continued education, and even sports—than was the case just a few decades ago.

For example, although the elderly have in the past been less computer literate than young people, that is changing rapidly. Users over fifty-five are currently the fastest-growing group on Facebook, and according to a March 2010 article in *AARP: The Magazine*, 450,000 Americans over sixty-five post their own blogs. As people accustomed to relying on communication technology grow older, they are not going to stop using it; and the generations that knew nothing of computers in youth will gradually disappear. The effects of wide usage of the Internet by elders may be profound, for online, age is not relevant or even, in many cases, revealed. Everyone meets there on equal terms; just as young teens are sometimes assumed be older, people whose physical appearance would characterize them as "old men" or "old women" are often assumed to be younger. Moreover, Internet contacts can go a long way toward easing the loneliness of elderly people who are isolated. Half of all women over seventy-five live alone, and many of them are physically unable to get around in their communities; some go for days at a time without seeing anyone. Social networking on the Web can make a huge difference in their well-being.

Just where is the milestone past which a person becomes "elderly"? For most statistical purposes, it remains sixty-five, but since the "normal" retirement age is rising, that has no actual significance. A poll reported by the Pew Research Center in July 2010 showed Americans think the average person becomes old at sixty-eight. But this figure, said the report, "masks big age-related difference in judgment about when old age begins. Those under 30 say the average person becomes old at

60, while those 65 and above push that threshold to 74. . . . There's one predominant theme that emerges from older survey respondents on the subject of old age: I myself haven't arrived there yet." Even among those older than seventy-five, only 35 percent said they felt old.

To be sure, elderly people often have physical limitations even if they are not seriously ill. But that does not mean that they cannot live productive, and in most cases contented, lives. While on one hand, those physically able are more active than was once typical of old age; on the other, technology is erasing the distinctions from younger people once imposed by aging bodies. Such tasks as laundry and cooking do not demand physical stamina anymore; almost anyone can move a meal from a freezer to a microwave oven. Someone who can no longer drive to the store can order virtually anything—including groceries—over the Internet with just a few clicks. A person whose eyesight is failing need not give up reading when e-books make it possible to enlarge fonts, and software exists to read books aloud. Cell phones, e-mail, and Web cams make it easy to stay in touch with friends and relatives who are busy or far away. Wearable pendants for summoning help in emergencies by pushing a button are now common. And just over the horizon are robots that are being developed to serve the disabled elderly in many ways, making it possible for them to do without human assistance in daily living.

In today's world, advocates assert, there is no reason to set older individuals apart from other adults merely on the basis of age. Additionally, some medical conditions that used to be attributed solely to aging are now known to be illnesses that can be prevented, or if unavoidable, can be treated if not cured. Since the elderly constitute a minority that everybody who lives past middle age will someday join, no one should underestimate their capabilities.

CHAPTER 1

How Do Negative Stereotypes Affect Americans' Perception of the Elderly?

Chapter Preface

As is often observed, American society idolizes youth. From their twenties onward, both women and men are dismayed by any signs of aging and seek to look younger. Those nearing or past forty consider it normal to keep their true age a secret. Entertainment and commercial promotion alike are focused on the young, while little respect is paid to the qualities developed over time by adults who have attained maturity. Unlike the people of cultures where age and wisdom are honored, Americans dread growing old. The result—and perhaps the partial cause—of this attitude is that they tend to have negative perceptions of the elderly.

In the minds of many and by the media, the elderly are often portrayed as weak, dependent, prone to confusion, and less capable than younger adults—in any case, past their prime. Those in the public eye, such as politicians, scientists, and movie stars, are viewed as exceptions and not thought of as "elderly" at all. Furthermore, having encountered such assumptions about old age all their lives, elderly people themselves frequently share these perceptions. The stereotype becomes a self-fulfilling prophecy that can even affect their health; if they expect to be incapacitated in old age, that in itself may make it happen.

Are the elderly really a special class, separate from the general population, that should be treated differently and judged by different standards? Many of them, especially those who have reached sixty in recent years, say not. Most older people do not want to be seen as different from other adults. Like anyone else, they are individuals, and some are more capable than others.

The bias against elderly people appears to be lessening. For one thing, they constitute a larger percentage of the population than they used to; life span has increased, and as the large "baby boomer" generation reaches retirement age, the ranks of the elderly population will continue to grow. For another, there is more tolerance of minorities in general than there was in the past, and more sensitivity to the use of words with negative connotations. As in the case of other minorities, an effort is being made to phase out such terms; many writers now prefer "older adults" to "elderly" wherever it is not too ambiguous, and "senior citizen" is being replaced by "elder." The website ElderTimes.org explains, "The term senior citizen does not tell us of the years of experience or wisdom older adults have accumulated that are of benefit to society. It does not convey the sense of tradition and learning that older adults can offer. The term 'elder' is much richer and more meaningful. . . . Elder is respectful. Elder gives deference to the years of accumulated knowledge and wisdom that comes from living."

And yet, however much respect is shown toward older adults and however successfully they are integrated into mainstream society, there is an obvious need for special provisions to meet their basic necessities. Declining health does prevent many from retaining the degree of independence younger adults enjoy, and at some point in old age, most need care. The unfortunate cannot cope with homelessness and hunger as well as young people can. Often those capable of holding jobs and in need of income cannot get work, either because of prejudice against older workers or simply because jobs are scarce. Additionally, the elderly are vulnerable to abuse, not so much from incapacity (except in the case of illness or dementia), but because they are presumed to be weak and are therefore targeted by con men and other abusers. It is generally felt that society has an obligation to protect people who can no longer fend for themselves, and there is no practical way to distinguish those who can from those who cannot. Also, almost everyone agrees that citizens who have worked and paid taxes all their lives are owed something.

Therefore, since it cannot be said that there should be no difference between the services provided to elders and those available to everyone, there must of necessity be an arbitrary dividing line between the elderly and the population at large. Furthermore, the mere fact of having fewer years left to live than younger people sets elders apart. But these distinctions have no bearing on how older adults should be perceived by others. Like all human beings, they should be viewed not as members of a class but as individuals.

Bias Against the Elderly Creates a Negative View of Aging

Thomas Day

Thomas Day specializes in long-term care planning and is the director of the National Care Planning Council.

American society in general glorifies youth and fears or even despises old age. This is not the case in many other societies where age is associated with wisdom, knowledge and special status.

We see evidence of this bias towards older Americans especially in the media. In films and on TV old people are very often depicted as weak, indecisive, bumbling or even comic. We laugh at their misdeeds and forgive their mistakes knowing in the back of our minds that they are old and can't help themselves. We view them not as capable as younger people. It is rarely that we see older people depicted as decisive, strong or as leaders. We see this same attitude with large corporations and government employers. At a certain age, employees are encouraged or expected to "retire" to a new phase of their lives where they are not required to work for a living any longer. Retirement is presumably a reward for many years of dedication and hard work, but the underlying philosophy is more likely based on the idea that older workers are no longer productive or useful.

As Americans age we fear the deterioration of our bodies and the possible lack of security due to low income—a byproduct of old age. Some people in our country fight old age through cosmetic surgery, use of supplements, aggressive weight loss programs or through overzealous physical training programs. Other people accept old age gracefully and adapt as well as they can. Still others refuse to grow old and resist aging by adopting social strategies such as denial, refusal to participate in life or becoming belligerent. (The angry old codger image).

Instead of taking the role as leaders in their families or in the community as is the case in some countries, the elderly in our country, even after successful careers in earlier years, simply become invisible. They waste their prodigious talents traveling, entertaining, socializing, watching TV or playing golf. They are rarely asked to assume responsible roles in the community. And unlike other cultures, older Americans often abandon themselves to control by other people, often their children and their health care providers. Instead of taking responsibility for their own decisions, they will rely on children or others to make decisions for them. Many of them seem to enjoy the role of becoming dependent on others. And it is all too often the case that family and others pander to this submissive role of the elderly and we begin treating them like children.

In films and on TV old people are very often depicted as weak, indecisive, bumbling or even comic.

This generally accepted perception of aging in our country has resulted in the elderly themselves and in the community at large regarding older people as less valuable than younger people. The assumption is that the elderly have lost the ability to think clearly, to learn new things and they are generally incapable of any physical activity other than walking or sitting. This attitude also carries over into the health treatment that older Americans receive.

Older Persons' Attitudes Towards Their Health

Many elderly buy into the notion that they themselves are no longer useful and as a result make little attempt to keep themselves healthy and active. After all, they are getting closer to the end of their lives and have no desire to try new things or to challenge themselves or to eat or exercise properly.

There is a great deal of anecdotal and research evidence that demonstrates older people can learn, can retain memory and can be actively involved in business and in the community. The lack of physical exercise, social involvement and mental stimulation in older Americans often leads to these people losing the ability to use their minds and their bodies. The older person's negative attitude towards aging becomes self-fulfilling.

Many reason that they have missed their opportunities in life when they were younger and it's too late to start over. As a result, many older people are intimidated by new ideas or by technology such as computers, not because they are incapable but simply because of their attitude. The idea of not being able to "teach an old dog new tricks" is in most cases an excuse. Obviously this mind-set of failure and inability to perform becomes self-fulfilling. Not surprisingly, depression and suicide are more common in the elderly than in the younger population.

Many elderly buy into the notion that they themselves are no longer useful.

The negative attitude towards aging on the part of an older person has a direct impact on that person's health. Many studies show that people who are physically active have less joint pain, lower blood pressure, less depression, fewer heart attacks and a lower incidence of cancer. Proper nutrition also has the same effect on the aging process; it delays the onset of debilitating illness or disability.

According to James S. Marks, M.D., M.P.H., director of the National Center for Chronic Disease Prevention and Health Promotion:

> "Research has shown that poor health does not have to be an inevitable consequence of growing older. Death is inevitable, but for many people, it need not be preceded by a slow, painful, and disability-ridden decline. Our nation will continue to age—that we cannot change—but we can delay and in many cases prevent illness and disability."

A study in 2000 from the *Journal of the American Geriatrics Society* reports that inactive women at age 65 have a life expectancy of 12.7 years whereas highly active, nonsmoking women at 65 have a life expectancy of 18.4 years. A report from the CDC [Centers for Disease Control and Prevention] indicates that very few older Americans get 30 minutes or more exercise for five days a week or more. The report states that up to 34% of adults age 65 to 74 are inactive and up to 44% or almost half of adults age 75 are inactive. A study from the U.S. Preventive Services Task Force reveals that regular exercise can reduce life-threatening falls in the elderly by 58%. Another study showed that regular exercise reduced pain and increased function in joints of older Americans suffering from osteoarthritis. . . . Yet another study found that strength training was as effective as medication in reducing depressive symptoms in older adults. Other studies from the Department of Health and Human Services support the idea that older people who are responsible for their own health and their own health decisions are healthier than people who rely on others to make decisions for them.

Ageism, Like Racism and Sexism, Should Be Challenged

Robert Butler, as told to Patrick Perry

Robert Butler is an expert in the field of aging and author of
The Longevity Revolution: The Benefits and Challenges of
Living a Long Life. *Patrick Perry is an author and frequent contributor to the* Saturday Evening Post.

Sounding a call to action, a renowned expert on aging examines the health, economic, and social challenges and opportunities of growing older in today's society.

As people live longer than ever, tough questions surface
about the impact of aging on our population as a whole. Can
we afford old age? How can we make the extra years productive personally and rewarding for society? Will Social Security
and Medicare collapse under the pressure of growing numbers
of retirees?

In his latest book *The Longevity Revolution: The Benefits
and Challenges of Living a Long Life*, Robert Butler, M.D., an
internationally recognized expert in the field of aging and gerontology, grapples with these issues and presents an agenda
for action. The founding director of the National Institute on
Aging and CEO of the International Longevity Center, Butler
calls for a "colossal public-private research initiative" to combat disease, gain a better understanding of the biology of aging, and improve health promotion and health care. The man
who coined the term "ageism" argues that the United States
has not made the much-needed research investment in aging.

Dealing with the Effects of Aging

The *Post* spoke to the Pulitzer Prize–winning author about his
latest book and what Americans can do to take advantage of
the unprecedented leap in human life expectancy.

Patrick Perry, "Spearheading the Longevity Revolution," *Saturday Evening Post*, July 1, 2008. Reproduced by permission.

What is the Longevity Revolution?

In Roman times, with the realities of infant mortality and women dying giving birth, the average life expectancy was about 20. In 1776, the average life expectancy in the United States was estimated by historical demographers to have been 35, with about two percent of the population over 65. By 1900, the average life expectancy was 47, with only four percent of the population over 65. By the end of the century, we suddenly have more than 12 percent with an average life expectancy essentially of 77. Nothing like this had happened in human history. It took 5,000 years to achieve. I call this unprecedented demographic transformation the Longevity Revolution.

I depend a lot on the media to sensitively discuss the issues of aging. Of course, we definitely need legislative support: Discrimination doesn't wantonly occur.

You've studied aging for more than 50 years and coined the term "ageism." American culture seems youth-oriented. As a society, are Americans increasingly afraid of getting older?

It's hard to answer that question with authority, but I can offer an impressionistic answer. We're a little more sensitive to aging than maybe we have been. I've had at least five calls from the press about John McCain, asking if he's too old to run for president, will he live long enough to live out his term, and should such an old person be elected president? I would remind them that Konrad Adenauer led post–World War Germany until age 87, while Charles de Gaulle was prime minister of post–World War France until age 78. Function is the issue, not age per se. I faced the same questions when Bob Dole ran [for U.S. president in 1996]. Many thought he would never outlive his presidency if elected. If he had been elected, he would have long since left the presidency and still be alive. While it's hard to give an objective measure, there may be some slight improvement.

How do you get society to come to confront these important issues?

Perception depends a lot on the media. How did the media get people to consider that there might actually be climate change and global warming? It took a long time. Maybe the movie *An Inconvenient Truth* helped tip the scale.

I depend a lot on the media to sensitively discuss the issues of aging. Of course, we definitely need legislative support: Discrimination doesn't wantonly occur. What can we do to improve the health of people? One issue that always seemed a very important part of people's fear of aging is disease and decrepitude. If we can finally eliminate Alzheimer's disease and frailty, people would look at aging in a very different way and wouldn't be so frightened by it.

Individually, we fear growing old. We don't want to think about it too much. I don't think we want to be morbidly preoccupied with aging, but we have to think about it some or we'll pay a personal price from lack of planning.

Does discrimination play a role in routine preventive screenings?

I think so. While uncommon, it can occur. Our preventive strategies tend to be oriented toward young people, as they should be. But they should be oriented toward old people as well. For example, take falling and breaking the hip or injuring your head. Falls are the number 12 cause of death among older people. How often do doctors encourage older patients to develop techniques to assure better balance? There are ways to practice balance so that you're not as likely to fall. How often does the doctor say "You've got to strengthen your thigh muscles—or quadriceps—to reduce the chance of falls?" Unfortunately, these issues are not part of the thinking of average doctors.

When asked, a 71-year-old woman said she would love to live to 100 but feared that she might outlive her resources. How do we address these issues?

That is a very important fear. Only half of American adults know the difference between a stock and a bond. There is enormous financial illiteracy. We need a better-educated population to learn at least the basics of economics and savings. We don't have a real savings rate in this country. In fact, it's almost the other way around: We have more indebtedness than savings. That contributes to the fear of outliving resources. Of course, we need to teach our children to think about finances. People should save all of their lives: they can't depend upon Social Security.

As a society, how are we going to be able to address that need?

We really have to take a "life span perspective" and teach children that they have responsibilities for their health and to save money. It can't just be the government that takes care of you in your old age; you have to prepare for it. Kids can be taught to invest; kids can be taught the difference between a stock and a bond; and kids can be put on exercise programs so they don't become overweight. As a doctor, I'm horrified to see ten-year-old children with adult-onset type 2 diabetes. It's terrible! Most of the responsibility for a decent old age rests with the individual and his family, not the government.

The longer that someone's been on the job, the more expensive employees typically become. It's attractive for businesses to replace them with younger workers at lower pay.

Millions of baby boomers are nearing 65. Are they prepared?

Baby boomers who have a 401(k)—and not everyone does—have about $40,000. It's hard to believe that's going to carry them through retirement. They're really facing a critical issue. Baby boomers, in my judgment, are a generation at risk because we can't solve all the many issues that affect and will affect them. They may be transformative and help generations that follow, but baby boomers, I'm afraid, are going to potentially suffer.

Obviously, many are going to have to work longer. In the book, you report on studies of older workers in the U.S., concluding that while reaction time may be slower, older workers demonstrated less absenteeism, higher job satisfaction, greater dependability, and experience. What stumbling blocks do employers face in hiring older workers?

Of course, the longer that someone's been on the job, the more expensive employees typically become. It's attractive for businesses to replace them with younger workers at lower pay. As a society, we may have to do some rethinking. Older people may have to be willing to take lower pay to preserve their jobs.

We might also change the way health insurance is paid. For example, the health insurer is often the first payer, not Medicare, even if it's a worker over 65. If that were to change by law, Medicare would become the first payer rather than health insurance. That would save employers a lot of money. We have to face the music that there are certain built-in financial disincentives that make it harder for employers to retain older workers. The payoff in the long run for society in general would be to change policies.

Is working longer associated with increased longevity?

Based on findings from studies we did years ago, it would appear that people who have a purpose in life—something to get up for that makes a difference—actually live longer and better than those who do not. It's also good for society that people continue to contribute on a volunteer basis.

Do workers need to exert extra effort to adapt to the changing work environment by learning new skills?

We're going to have to be more self-inventive and learn new skills. Norway and Australia, as I write in the book, provide kind of sabbaticals for people so they have a chance to build new careers. We need to give people a shot at being able to change their status as workers in society. Of course, with all the emerging technological developments in the workplace, it's good to develop multiple skills.

In the future, we will need more specialists in geriatrics to meet the demands. How can we provide incentives to young doctors to enter the field?

There's no question that finances play a role. On average, a medical student leaves medical school with about $150,000 worth of debt, so it's very attractive to enter a specialty that makes more money. Geriatrics is not one of those fields. In Europe, most medical education is public and free. Students don't graduate with debts. In this country, South Carolina, for example, has a debt-forgiveness program for doctors who go into geriatrics. Last March, California Senator Barbara Boxer introduced legislation—The Caring for An Aging America Act—to do the same thing on a national level, so it would apply to all states.

We've read about problems with nursing homes and elder abuse for years. Why do these problems persist?

There's a scandal almost every couple of years. It goes back again to age discrimination. The thinking: These are just old people—we've got more important ways to spend our money, so we don't have to worry about them—is part of it. The nursing home lobby is pretty effective in delivering a positive impression of the industry and in getting Uncle Sam to pay them more money.

How does America compare to the rest of the world in treatment of its elders?

It varies. We have a lot of romance, thinking the grass is greener on the other side. Problems with prejudice and discrimination against older people exist in other countries, too. We may have a little more idolatry for youth than perhaps other countries do, which may have its disadvantages. We have a more superior medical research establishment than most Europeans and nations worldwide—which, of course, benefits older people. However, we don't have long-term care insurance coverage like Germany, Japan, and the Netherlands. We are definitely not where we should be. . . .

They should also try to help their fellow man. Not to sound sappy and sentimental, I think that we all should have some relationship to each other and concern for each other.

What can individuals do to contribute to the revolution in adjusted needs of an aging society?

They should read and think about it. They should also try to help their fellow man. Not to sound sappy and sentimental. I think that we all should have some relationship to each other and concern for each other. Older people should volunteer more, such as helping our children. In a country with an abysmal educational record where kids from the perspective of math and science rank about number 18 among nations, people with skills in math and science could make a real contribution in after-school enrichment programs to help kids. . . .

Has your perspective on aging changed as you have aged?

There are no secrets. For a long time, I thought that maybe I'll discover things that never dawned on me. One thing that is interesting to me is that the fear of death goes down for whatever reason. You would think that since you're closer to death on a realistic basis and uneasy about the prospect of the unknown, you'd be more troubled as you grow older. That has not happened for me at all. I feel less threatened by the end of life than I perhaps did when I was 35.

Negative Stereotypes About the Elderly Are Formed in Early Childhood

Jamie Hanlon

Jamie Hanlon is a public affairs associate at the University of Alberta.

Sometimes inspiration comes from the strangest of places.

For Sheree Kwong See, it happened during a testing session with a subject while conducting a study on language and cognitive changes in the elderly. Kwong See was explaining the test to the research participant who reacted to the instructions in a quite unexpected manner.

"She said, 'I can't do that. I'm old,'" said Kwong See.

But after Kwong See spent some time comforting and encouraging the participant, Kwong See and the woman were amazed to see that the woman who said she would be unable to complete the test scored significantly better than expected. And her initial reaction gave Kwong See the idea to research how beliefs about the elderly—specifically in terms of their perceived abilities—affect them and others.

As part of a Social Sciences and Humanities Research Council [of Canada]-funded study, Kwong See partnered with fellow University of Alberta researcher Elena Nicoladis to investigate the early beginnings of stereotypes about aging. They measured the reactions of young children after being quizzed on vocabulary words by either an older or younger adult, in order to assess whether toddlers have a bias against older people.

Jamie Hanlon, "Research Indicates Toddlers Can Become Ageists by Three," *University of Alberta ExpressNews*, August 19, 2009. Copyright © 2009 by University of Alberta ExpressNews. Reproduced by permission.

The results, which are to be published in an upcoming [2009] issue of *Educational Gerontology*, proved to be unsettling. Kwong See's study revealed that negative stereotypes about cognitive ability in old age may be held by some children between the ages of two and three, which could adversely affect them when they are older.

"We've been able to show that even young children have beliefs about older people's abilities," said Kwong See. "We're seeing what we could call ageism by about age three."

The researchers assessed bias by making use of a tendency of children when learning words to assume a new word refers to something they do not already know. "We gave them a word they do not know, a non-word such as 'dax,'" said Kwong See. "We were looking to see if they're going to say it's the thing they don't know."

Negative biases can be damaging in [children's] interaction with and treatment of the elderly throughout their lives and in their own self-concept as they grow older.

With the younger person, children readily identified the unfamiliar object. However, with the older person, children were more hesitant in pointing out the unfamiliar object. Their uncertainty, says Kwong See, may be related to their perceptions of the older person as someone who is perhaps confused or not as competent as a younger person. "They're making that shift where, all of a sudden, the older person isn't as good a teacher or they're not as reliable a source of information as a young person is," she said.

Exposure to Older Adults Reduces Bias

In analyzing the results, the researchers noted that children whose parents had declared that their children were frequently exposed to older adults reacted differently. These children showed a more positive bias toward the older person. They reacted as if the older person was more knowledgeable about words than the younger person.

"If you are interacting with 'nana' more frequently, you'll start to see that she's a pretty good teacher of words even though she's old," said Kwong See. "When you have little contact, dominant negative cultural stereotypes emerge. You think an older person isn't as alert or in-the-know as a young person and maybe is not as good a teacher."

However, before making frantic trips to grandmother's house to curb the bias, Kwong See cautions that this is not the sole factor from which these biases can develop.

"[Children] are getting negative images of aging from cartoons, from their storybooks, from watching how other people interact with seniors," she said. "But, they also start picking up some of the positive images as well if they get lots of good interactions."

The long-term implications for these negative biases can be damaging in their interaction with and treatment of the elderly throughout their lives and in their own self-concept as they grow older, says Kwong See.

"Eventually those same children, once they know those stereotypes, may find that the stereotypes become a self-fulfilling prophecy," said Kwong See. "They will become their stereotypes about themselves as they grow older."

Negative Stereotypes About the Elderly Are Widespread and Damaging

Kay Lazar

Kay Lazar is a reporter for the Boston Globe.

When you think about aging, what words and images come to mind? Wrinkled, forgetful, maybe feeble?

You might want to rethink those, and try spry, wise, and distinguished, because our negative perceptions of our elders may have adverse effects on our own long-term health, according to a growing body of research.

Scientists are increasingly linking negative stereotypes about older adults to a number of health problems, from memory impairments to increased risk of heart disease and even a shortened life span. With elders often portrayed as the dentures, wrinkle cream, and incontinence segment of our youth-obsessed society, negative messages about aging can be pernicious and long-lasting, specialists say.

One recent study, by Yale University psychologist Becca Levy, tracked a group of 440 adults, from 1968 until 2007. It found that those who expressed gloomy views about elders when they were younger were much more likely to suffer a heart attack, stroke, or other cardiac problem 30 years later, compared to those who held more benign opinions. Specifically, 25 percent of those in the negative age-stereotype group had experienced a heart problem, compared to just 13 percent in the positive age-stereotype group, even taking into account variables such as blood pressure, smoking, and cholesterol levels.

Our negative perceptions of our elders may have adverse effects on our own long-term health.

The findings build on Levy's earlier work, which revealed that negative images of aging can increase stress, while positive ones can be calming. Other researchers have linked high stress levels to heart disease.

After scrutinizing stereotypes and their effects on health for the past 15 years, Levy believes that age-related stereotypes, more so than other types, get ingrained at an early age and then are not consciously reevaluated as we get older.

"If you look at gender stereotypes, for instance, girls who are exposed to stereotypes of females are more likely to question them because they are female," Levy said. "But age stereotypes are different because children are taking them in long before they think of themselves as aging."

When it comes to aging, Americans apparently harbor deep-seated and uncomfortable feelings.

Harvard social psychologist Mahzarin Banaji has long explored people's unconscious beliefs about a variety of sensitive subjects—from race, gender, and weight to religion and aging—and has found negative biases about aging to be among the strongest and most widely held. Roughly 80 percent of the thousands of people Banaji has studied over the past decade in a Web-based test have indicated an "automatic" preference for young people over older ones.

Banaji measures how people respond to images and words flashed so quickly on a computer screen that they don't have time to think through their answers and instead must give their subliminal, and researchers believe, truer feelings. What she found is that "even elderly people themselves show the [negative] age bias as strongly as young people do."

The idea that bad thoughts about aging can adversely affect health rings true for Dr. Thomas Perls, who has long studied people who live past 100 years old. "Centenarians tend to be a very optimistic group, they tend not to dwell on things that were stressful, and they are able to let go," said Perls, founder and director of the New England Centenarian Study at Boston University School of Medicine.

Among the elders Perls is tracking is Sarah Bottrell, a 105-year-old retired high school teacher in Marquette, Mich. A self-described optimist who has outlived all of her relatives, Bottrell said she doesn't dwell on the past, sings in her church choir, and has a "marvelous" circle of friends.

One other point—she doesn't "concentrate" on age.

"Ever since the '60s, when the country started acting crazy, that's when they started concentrating on people's age," Bottrell said. "In growing up, we never talked about ages. What difference does it make as long as you are doing OK? It doesn't make any difference whether you are 65 or 25."

The power of positive thinking when it comes to aging may have a parallel in the negative territory. Increasingly, researchers are finding that negative biases may become self-fulfilling prophesies.

North Carolina State University psychologist Tom Hess concluded in a 2009 study that elders who thought they should perform poorly on memory tests actually scored worse than seniors who did not believe negative stereotypes about aging and memory loss.

Hess gave adults ages 60 to 82 specific information that suggested an age bias, such as telling them that the researchers were trying to understand why younger and older adults perform differently on memory tests—and then asked each to write down his or her age. These elders did not do as well as those who were simply told that adults of various ages performed similarly on the test.

"If people buy into stereotypes of aging, they may stay away from tasks involving memory because they are concerned they may not be able to do well," Hess said. And that, he said, can feed on itself, perhaps affecting a person's future ability to recall information.

At the University of Kansas, researcher Mary Lee Hummert found in a 2006 study of baby boomers, ages 48 to 62, that those who thought of themselves as older tended to have poorer recall on memory tests than those who identified with younger people. "We do internalize very early in life that youth is better than old age, and it doesn't leave us, even though it is modified," Hummert said. "And it does affect how we live our lives and make choices."

Those choices might help explain why some people, like Bottrell, the 105-year-old from Michigan, have lived so long.

Levy, the Yale researcher, has found that people older than 50 with more positive self-perceptions of aging, measured up to 23 years earlier, lived 7.5 years longer than those with less positive views. This advantage, documented in a 2002 study, held true, even after other factors were taken into account, such as age, gender, and socioeconomic status.

"It would be nice, with baby boomers becoming older, that stereotypes would become more positive," Levy said, "but we haven't seen that yet."

Positive Perceptions of Old Age Should Be Cultivated by the Young

Ilan Shrira

Ilan Shrira is a social psychologist at the University of Florida in Gainesville.

Think of the last time you went to buy a funny birthday card for a friend. Can you remember what some of the cards said, what their punch lines were? Chances are many of them joked about old age leading to memory loss, senility, loss of sexuality, or physical disabilities. Each card may have looked like innocent fun, but taken as a whole, our regular exposure to these negative assumptions about old age leads us to implicitly accept them.

Stereotypes of the elderly are stronger and more negative than we realize, often expressed in subtle and seemingly harmless ways, escaping our notice.

Consider a recent Snickers commercial that depicts octogenarian [a person in her eighties] actress Betty White playing hard-nosed tackle football. Its humor is driven by everyone's expectation that a woman her age could never do this. We know the commercial's meant to be tongue-in-cheek, so where's the harm in that? The problem is that portrayals like this reinforce the underlying assumption that elderly people are frail and helpless (while ironically, portraying Betty White as tough).

Negative stereotypes of the elderly are by no means universal—they depend on how a society views closeness to extended family, dependence on others, and traditional ideals (for example, that being old and wise is something to aspire to). These values are de-emphasized in Western cultures, where elderly people are treated especially badly.

Stereotypes of the elderly are stronger and more negative than we realize, often expressed in subtle and seemingly harmless ways.

Young People Will Someday Be Old

When we become aware of prejudice, we're usually concerned with how it affects the people who are targeted. However, negative stereotypes of the elderly also carry a terrible cost for those who *hold* the stereotypes, in a way that no other kind of prejudice does. Unlike markers of race, disability, social class, and other stigmas, *old age is the only group that everyone will someday belong to* (if you're lucky, that is). Hence, young people who have negative perceptions of the elderly will eventually develop negative perceptions of themselves. Negative perceptions of the elderly don't just magically disappear once you become part of the demographic; deeply held assumptions tend to be persistent.

We also know that when people come to accept the negative stereotypes directed at their own group, this can short-circuit their thinking and cause the stereotypes to become self-fulfilling prophecies. For example, imagine someone who's an average math student but believes herself to be very bad at it. Although she has the ability to do well, every time she takes a math exam or is asked to calculate a restaurant tip, she gets anxious and makes mistakes—so that her assumptions about herself wind up getting confirmed. A similar process occurs when elderly people buy into the assumptions they see on birthday cards and in mainstream culture.

Elderly people who hold negative beliefs about aging— such as the belief that mental and physical health inevitably get worse with age; or that things like arthritis, difficulty sleeping, and heart disease are normal aspects of aging—end up performing worse on short-term memory and hearing acuity tests. More alarmingly, long-running studies find that people who hold these beliefs are more likely to suffer heart attacks and strokes, take longer to recover from them, and have a significantly lower life expectancy. These outcomes are not caused by poorer health to begin with, or personality differences, but instead are directly predicted by positive vs. negative beliefs about aging. . . .

How can these beliefs actually shape our physical and mental health? What are the mechanisms involved?

A big way is through a person's health maintenance behaviors. People who believe that health can be improved through a better diet, exercise, and getting regular physicals—these are examples of positive aging beliefs—are more likely to maintain these activities and stay healthier in the long run. They're also more likely to discuss health issues with their doctor and to take their prescribed medications. In contrast, people who believe that aging inevitably leads to deteriorating health are less motivated to engage in health-promoting behaviors, believing them to be pointless (and ultimately causing their assumptions about aging to get confirmed).

Negative Stereotypes on Age Produce Stress

Negative self-stereotypes are also harmful because they produce stress. For instance, exposing elderly people to negative age stereotypes—like the jokes you see on birthday cards—triggers physiological stress responses (e.g., increases in heart rate and blood pressure), which damages health over time. When you consider how frequently these stereotypes get transmitted in everyday life, this extra stress is sure to increase the risk of cardiovascular disease and other health problems.

Despite their effects on older people, holding these stereotypes doesn't impair the functioning of young people, who don't see them as applying to themselves. In fact, holding these beliefs may actually be empowering to young people—making them feel healthier, more competent, and better off by comparison. This sense of superiority is likely a big reason people cling to these beliefs.

The aversion toward old age is also driven by our fear of it—at the prospect of losing our independence, appearing vulnerable, changes in our appearance, and death. However, spurning old age, while it can be temporarily comforting, ends up being a destructive way to deal with our fears.

Exposing elderly people to negative age stereotypes—like the jokes you see on birthday cards—triggers physiological stress responses.

A first step to changing our assumptions is to simply be aware of the extreme negativity that gets associated with old age, and learn not to get caught up in it. Even more important, we need to cultivate positive beliefs about aging, since even small reminders of them can make a big difference. For example, when elderly people are briefly shown positive stereotype words—such as *accomplished, enlightened, insightful, nurturing, wise*—this immediately improves their all-around functioning: producing better memory, reduced stress, greater self-confidence, and more positive perceptions of aging.

These positive perceptions can be sustained in the long run as well. One way is by creating a mental image of what you *want* to be like in your 70s and 80s, a realistic version of your best possible self. By considering your best future self, "old age" will no longer be this distant event that's seen through the lens of our cultural stereotypes. Instead, envisioning your future self is a great way to clarify which long-term goals are important to you (e.g., good health, good relationships), motivating you to pursue these goals and giving you a sense of control over your future. (Tip: *Writing* about your best future self is even more effective than just imagining it.)

We're fully capable of improving our perceptions about aging (and thus making them more realistic). Doing so will require active maintenance strategies, though, given all the negativity we're exposed to about it. To continue to passively accept this mentality is dangerous—we need to accept that our beliefs are integral to our health and well-being in later life.

In China the Elderly Are Honored and Admired

Kelly Clady-Giramma

Kelly Clady-Giramma is a staff acupuncturist at Canyon Ranch Spa in Lenox, Massachusetts.

When Americans think about what it means to grow old, they often have negative associations such as wasting away in loneliness in a convalescent home, having limited financial resources, being in constant pain, suffering from memory lapses or even Alzheimer's [disease]—being generally unwell and unhappy. Ask a typical Chinese person what they associate with aging and they likely will paint a much different picture: being surrounded by family members of all ages, being respected by family and society, enjoying playing cards every day with neighbors their own age, having a certain amount of aches and pains but not being incapacitated, taking grandchildren to school by bike and enjoying leisure time that they didn't have in their youth.

These contrasting stereotypical pictures of aging do not always mirror reality. They do, nonetheless, illustrate the large influence society can have on an individual's aging process. Having spent most of the past three years living in China, I was affected deeply by the love and adoration people have there for the elderly. Although many Chinese have adopted more Western, quick-paced lifestyles in the past 10 to 15 years, they still adhere to the Confucian [referring to the teachings of Chinese philosopher Confucius] ideal of honoring their elders. They don't merely just give up their bus seats to older folks, they integrate them into every aspect of life. I believe it is this attitude in large part that accounts for the fact that seniors in China, often with deep wrinkles and weathered faces from years of struggle and hardship, still have vibrancy and serene contentedness I've rarely observed in their American peers.

Young people in China seem much less assured and confident than their parents and grandparents despite the fact that most of them have grown up with material comfort previously unknown to past generations. These fortunate young Chinese, *unfortunately*, rarely have the time to enjoy themselves. From the time Chinese children begin preschool, life is all about passing various exams and pleasing parents and teachers. There is little time for true relaxation until college which, according to all my Chinese friends, is far less stressful than their elementary and high school years. After college, they begin the serious business of finding work in China's ever-competitive job market, next comes a spouse and then that long-awaited grandchild who will be doted on and sacrificed to the *nth* degree by both parents and two sets of grandparents. If these goals are not fulfilled by age 30 or so (earlier for women), they will be looked down upon a bit by all but the most liberal-minded families.

Seniors in China, often with deep wrinkles and weathered faces from years of struggle and hardship, still have vibrancy and serene contentedness.

Fast-forward to retirement. Assuming that a person in their 60s in China has at least one responsible adult child on whom to rely, they can finally live a little. (It should be noted, however, that childless Chinese run a similar risk to their American counterparts, in that governmental and pension support is not as much as it used to be in the old days of communism. The proverbial Chinese "iron rice bowl" has indeed been broken by current-day capitalistic economic practices.) Old people are seen in China as offering a lot of experience and wisdom, and they are respected for having survived so long.

The Race Does Not Necessarily Belong to the Swiftest

Survival is a concept not taken lightly throughout Chinese history. This probably is the reason why Chinese traditionally didn't mark birthdays until they turned 60 years old. To this day, grandparents get big parties with a lot of to-do and children usually are just given a bowl of special noodles (a sign of long life) to mark their far less auspicious birthdays. The attitude is "Anyone can be young; it takes talent to be old!" A person's 80th birthday is believed to be the pinnacle of life that everyone aspires to and every birthday after that becomes more and more special.

What a contrast this is to our own adrenaline-, youth- and speed-addicted society. To slow down here in any way, even temporarily, implies weakness and inferiority. It is interesting to note that, according to TCM [traditional Chinese medicine] medical theory, children are "pure *yang*," a fact that anyone who has tried to chase a toddler around can attribute to! It is a misnomer, however, to assume that old people must be "pure *yin*." The whole point of life, according to Chinese medicine, is to try to retain as much of your *yang* energy, vitality and health as possible throughout every stage of life. (This is why those same hyperactive toddlers need to sleep so much!) What may perplex some adrenaline junkies is that the only way to have any *yang* (warm, energetic, active) energy left over when you get old is by balancing it with *yin* (restorative, cooling) activities and behaviors *before* you get old. Rather than the theory "use it or lose it," we might substitute instead with "abuse it (your body) and lose it!"

The intention of Chinese medicine is to provide tools for cultivating healthy *yang qi* [life force] and vitality. The Taoist sages who originally laid down the precepts for Chinese medicine wanted a way to achieve immortality. They weren't concerned with remaining young per se, they simply wanted to remain healthy and live a long, and possibly indefinite, life. The three main ways to do this, they believed, were through proper diet, using medicinal herbs and learning to strengthen inner *qi* through mind-body exercises such as *tai chi* and *qigong*. . . .

In China, beauty is not something which is merely confined to the young, though there is tremendous pressure on young women and men to be attractive. In fact, it often is a requirement for gainful employment these days. Older generations are seen as having inner strength and beauty which gives them a sense of pride and dignity.

Older Chinese people preserve their vital *qi* with many health-promoting strategies. They frequently take tonic herbs such as ginseng (*ren shen*), reishi mushroom, cordyceps (*dong chong xia cao*) or the formula *jin cui shen qi wan* to preserve kidney *qi*. Another phenomenon, which anyone who has traveled to China has witnessed, is that many older people do *tai chi* or other outdoor exercise for an hour or more per day, come rain or shine. The idea of being fit is not reserved for the young. In fact, exercise is a luxury for which most Chinese in their 20s and 30s cannot find the time, whereas their grandparents have ample time to while away the hours stretching and doing *qigong* or *tai chi* in the public parks. Many Chinese people in their 70s and 80s can put young American yoga enthusiasts to shame with their muscular strength and joint flexibility. I commonly saw people two generations older than me kick one leg up to their nose with grace and ease I haven't personally experienced since I was 25!

The Chinese Do Not Fight Against Getting Older

In contrast to China's reverence for the old, America's obsession with youth comes in large part from an inability to accept the impermanence of life. TCM theory states that human beings are merely one aspect of nature and thus go through the same phases of birth, growth, decline and death. The Chinese know this and don't fight tooth and nail against getting older the way Americans are prone to doing. It would be unthinkable for a Chinese woman in her 60s to contemplate plastic surgery to erase facial lines. The face throughout Chinese culture has been thought of as the canvas for character and personality. To artificially take away these character lines, which elderly people in China often view as their badge of experience, would be absurd. They are far more likely to be concerned with maintaining a healthy head of hair which, in keeping with Chinese medical theory, shows their good blood and kidney essence. This is why both older men and women often take *he shou wu* (literally "black-haired Mr. He") to nourish their hair, and why it's not uncommon for people to color their hair with black shoe polish! Vanity, as with beauty, would appear to also affect all generations.

Old people are seen in China as offering a lot of experience and wisdom, and they are respected for having survived so long.

Hopefully more and more Americans can learn to appreciate these Chinese ideas about graceful aging. The Chinese seem to understand that by taking care of their health in their younger years—staying socially involved with friends and family, taking time on a daily basis to rest and relax, and finding stimulating ways to use their minds and bodies—it is indeed possible to achieve a kind of longevity. It may not be the immortality sought by the Taoist sages, but it seems a much better quality of life than what's often practiced in the West. I'd like to think that I'll be taking my grandkids back and forth to school by bike like the Chinese when I'm in my 70s. If not, maybe I'll move to China so I can play Mahjong, do *tai chi* with my friends and get a little respect!

The ancient world, in many ways infinitely more wise than our own, acknowledged that the entirety of creation was in a process of ebb and flow, from un-manifest potentiality to manifest existence. Our planet exhibits this dynamic to us in the perennial cycle of the seasons (the five phases) in periods of birth, growth, maturity, decline and quiescence. We, too, according to the precepts of Chinese medicine, participate in this same rhythm of being and nonbeing in our individual lives. The Western world seemingly has harnessed its wagon to the stars, ever looking upward and outward from *terra firma* [solid earth]. Nevertheless, we are rooted here, and it is to that native soil—that nourishing feminine matrix—that each of us must, in due course, return.

In China, beauty is not something which is merely confined to the young.

Can we here in the West learn to acknowledge, like the Chinese, that each step of the journey is of equal significance? Can we learn from them how to mature gracefully, with dignity, embracing a way of life that supports the elderly, respects wisdom and celebrates aging? Most importantly, can we surrender our fear of impermanence and our desperate grasping after an eternity of youth?

CHAPTER 2

Are Elderly People Unhappy with Their Lives?

Overview: Research About Happiness in Old Age Yields Conflicting Results

Jeanna Bryner

Jeanna Bryner is the managing editor of LiveScience, a website devoted to science news.

Aging brings wrinkles, sagging bodies and frustrating forgetfulness. But getting older is not all bad for many people. Mounting evidence suggests aging may be a key to happiness. There is conflicting research on the subject, however, and experts say it may all boil down to this: Attitude is everything.

Older adults tend to be more optimistic and to have a positive outlook on life than their younger, stressed counterparts, research is finding. The results take on more meaning in light of the ongoing increase in life expectancy.

In one study, the average number of years a 30-year-old in the United States could expect to live increased 5.4 years for men and 3.6 years for women between 1970 and 2000. During that same time period, men gained 6.8 years of happy life and shed 1.4 unhappy years. Women chalked up 1.3 happy years, but the number of unhappy years didn't change for them, according to research published in 2008 by Yang Yang, a sociologist at the University of Chicago.

Her work suggests that an increase in years of happy life for the 65-plus age group accompanied the increase in life expectancy on average.

The big question, of course, is why seniors are happier.

Rose-Colored Memories

A more recent study by another team of researchers, published this month [April 2010] in the journal *Cortex*, suggests one reason: Older adults remember the past through a rosy lens.

Older adults tend to be more optimistic and to have a positive outlook on life than their younger, stressed counterparts.

The researchers recorded brain activity using fMRI [functional magnetic resonance imaging] scans while young and older adults viewed a series of photos with positive and negative themes, such as a victorious skier and a wounded soldier.

Results showed in the older adult brain, there were strong connections between emotion-processing regions of the brain and those known to be important for successful formation of memories, particularly when processing positive information. The same strong connections weren't found for the younger participants.

It's also becoming apparent to researchers that being old could lend itself to optimism. In one recent study, both old and young participants were shown virtual faces portraying sadness, anger, fear and happiness. Eye-tracking technology revealed the participants aged 18 to 21 focused on the fearful faces, while those aged 57 to 84 zeroed in on the happy faces, avoiding the angry ones.

The researchers—writing in a 2006 issue of the journal *Psychology and Aging*—think that as a person's life expectancy decreases, they might focus on what makes them feel good now rather than focusing on the negative.

Aging can bring more cheer as people become more comfortable with themselves and their role in society, according to another study published in 1989 by Walter R. Gove, professor of sociology, emeritus, at Vanderbilt University in Tennessee.

Older adults enjoy life in general it turns out. In a Pew Research Center survey of 2,969 adults in 2009, seven in ten respondents ages 65 and older said they were enjoying more time with their family. About two-thirds reported more time for hobbies, more financial security and not having to work as benefits of old age. About six in ten said they get more respect and feel less stress than when they were younger; and just over half cited more time to travel and to do volunteer work.

Contrary Findings

But others are skeptical of the link between happiness and growing older.

"The notion that those in old age are happiest is misleading," said Richard [A.] Easterlin, a professor of economics at the University of Southern California. "It is based on comparing people of different ages who are the same in terms of income, health, family life."

Easterlin added, "When you take account of the fact that older people have lower incomes than younger [individuals], are less healthy, and more likely to be living alone, then the old are less happy, which is exactly what you'd expect."

In fact, scientists have found that as people age, their health declines and social networks atrophy (as peers die), which can make the elderly less happy.

Even if one does succumb to age's dark side, health and happiness don't always go hand in hand. It's all about attitude, a study published back in 2005 found. The researchers examined 500 Americans age 60 to 98 who had dealt with cancer, heart disease, diabetes, mental health conditions or a range of other problems. Despite their ills, participants rated their degree of successful aging an average of 8.4 on a scale from 1 to 10 (best score). Other research out that year suggested the sick and disabled are just as happy as the rest of us.

All About Attitude

Research by the University of Chicago's Yang suggests that attitude about life, and thus happiness, is partly shaped by the era in which a person is born. For instance, she has found for those born in the 1900s depression declined with age while happiness increased more with age. And individuals born between the Great Depression and the end of World War II were more likely to say they are very happy compared with early baby boomers.

As people age, their health declines and social networks atrophy (as peers die), which can make the elderly less happy.

Happiness in old age could come down to how one stacks up to same-age peers or one's own expectations—say you're used to breakfast on a silver platter and when you get older you can only afford the basic English muffin. It turns out, individuals who adapt the best to changes also have the highest expected levels of happiness, according to the Population Reference Bureau [a nonprofit organization that tracks population trends].

Despite the conflicting findings about aging and happiness, the good news is that there doesn't appear to be a limit to how much happiness one can achieve in one's life.

"Most people desire happiness," Easterlin told LiveScience. "To my knowledge, no one has identified a limit to attainable happiness."

Retirement Leads Many to Feel That Their Lives Lack Purpose

Lillian B. Rubin

Lillian B. Rubin is a sociologist and psychotherapist. She is the author of twelve books and sold her first painting at the age of eighty-two.

"I was tired of working so hard, doing the same thing for so many years, so I retired a couple of years ago, figuring this was my chance at the golden years," says a seventy-two-year-old, his words etched in bitterness. "It was okay for a while, but all the 'fun' stuff doesn't seem like fun anymore, so now what? There's got to be something more than waking up wondering what the hell you're going to do with your day." He pauses, looks out the window at a view that would make anyone smile, turns pained eyes back to me, and snorts, "The golden years? They've gotta be kidding! If this is gold what's brass?"

In 1979 I published a book that included a chapter titled "What Am I Going to Do with the Rest of My Life?" Then, I was writing about women who, at forty, found themselves facing a frighteningly empty future. "Pretty much the whole of adult life was supposed to be around helping your husband and raising your children," exclaimed a forty-two-year-old woman who epitomized the dilemma of that era. "I mean, I never thought about what happens to the rest of life. Then all of a sudden, he doesn't need your help anymore and the children are raised. Now what?"

Much has changed in the intervening decades. . . . In the mid-twentieth century, when American life expectancy hovered around sixty-five, forty was on the cusp of middle age; questions about the "rest of life" presumed something like twenty more years, and it was mainly women who asked them. Men knew what the rest of their lives would bring. If they were lucky enough to live to retirement, they'd get a party, a gold watch, and not much time to enjoy it. Now [in 2007] a man who reaches the age of sixty-five can expect to live into his early eighties, a woman even later. . . .

Without work, without something to structure their days, . . . something that signals that [elderly individuals] still have a place in the world, life is stripped of much of its meaning.

Now What?

As we live longer, healthier lives, the question "Now what?" comes later, for some at sixty, for others not until seventy or more. But no matter how delayed, the question will arise with the same inevitability that death itself arrives on our doorstep. It makes no difference what our station is, whether high or low, we will all stand at the abyss as, by the very nature of living so long, we are forced to look into a future we cannot know and confront the combination of hope and fear that accompanies that reality.

"I wouldn't know what else to do," said Mike Wallace, the renowned television journalist, when, at eighty-eight, he was asked when he might leave the show at which he'd worked since 1968. When, a short time later, he suddenly announced his retirement without explanation, his former producer, Don Hewitt, speaking from his own experience, explained, "You get to a certain age . . . and you're not as gung ho as you thought you were going to be. But you hang onto *who you were* [italics added] because you don't know any better." To *who you were*, not *what you do*, because, as is so often the case, what you do becomes who you are. . . .

For lack of a better alternative, many people remain on the job well beyond what was once the accepted retirement age. Some, generally professional women and men who find satisfaction in their work and whose identity is closely tied to it, do so out of choice.

"I love my job; I love to teach; I can't imagine giving it up," exclaims a seventy-six-year-old college professor. Then, with a rueful smile, "Well, I guess the day will come when it won't be my choice, won't it? I can't imagine life without it."

Many more stay in the workforce or return to it after retirement out of need, sometimes economic, sometimes psychological, often a combination of both. . . . While their middle-aged children dream of a life beyond the rat race, one-third of their "retired" parents are back in the workforce, and two-thirds of those say they're there at least as much out of desire as economic need. During their working years, they looked forward to retirement with fantasies about all the things they couldn't do when they were working, whether going fishing, playing golf, remodeling the kitchen, or spending more time with the grandchildren. Then reality hit.

Just Keeping Busy

From the attorney to the truck driver, from the homemaker to the executive, the complaints are the same. Without work, without something to structure their days, something that marks the difference between Sunday and Monday, something that signals that they still have a place in the world, life is stripped of much of its meaning.

"Okay, so I pick my grandchildren up from school two days a week, and I love the time we have together. But what about the rest of the time?" asks a seventy-four-year-old retired social worker. "Sure, I keep busy, but that's just what it is—keeping busy. It doesn't have a lot of meaning, if you know what I mean."

The pleasures they'd looked forward to are indeed pleasurable, but not quite enough to still the restlessness that sets in—the sense that there must be something more—or to quiet the internal voice that asks so insistently: *Now what?*

"I used to think life would be perfect if I could play golf every day," remarks a seventy-six-year-old former salesman. "What can I tell you? Now I know that even if I did, there'd still be too many days in the week. I mean, I love it but . . ." His words trail off, as if searching for a way to avoid the thought he doesn't want to speak.

"But what?" I coach.

A deep sigh. "I don't know what to say; it's just not enough. It's not a life, that's all."

Go to any mall in America that houses stores like Home Depot, Wal-Mart, Target, Costco, and all the other retail outlets that eagerly hire older workers, and you'll see formerly retired women and men on the floor, usually doing jobs well below their capacity. It's a good deal for the companies. Older workers, unlike their baby boomer children, have little sense of entitlement. They don't complain, don't ask for anything, and are more reliable than younger workers. If that isn't enough to soothe any manager's anxious heart, retirees are happy to work part-time, which means they don't qualify for benefits—a big boost to the company's bottom line.

It sounds like exploitation, and it is. But in this case, what's good for business also works for those in need, who have few or no options. And indeed there are few for the older people who looked forward to retirement, thought it would be a walk on the sunny side, only to find themselves on a cold and lonely path. Even if they wanted to, they can't go back to the job they left, and they're not likely to find another one like it. So they take what they can get.

Tired of Retirement

"I retired a couple of years ago because I thought it was time to stop working and start living," says a seventy-year-old former forklift operator. "But after a couple of years, it got pretty damn old. My wife got tired of me moping around the house with nothing to do. I mean, how often can you tune up the car or fix the damn stopped drain? I just couldn't take it anymore. I woke up one morning and thought, Christ, if this is life, what's being dead like? Don't get me wrong, I don't love this job I've got now, but at least I'm back out in the world, and that's a lot better than sitting around the house drinking beer and wondering what I'm going to do today." Then he added, with a wry smile, "The extra cash doesn't hurt either."

It's a story I heard repeatedly in one version or another, including during a recent appearance on a local radio talk show. We weren't five minutes into a discussion about retirement and what it means today before the phone lines were jammed with women and men wanting to speak their experience about the difficulty of finding meaning in a life so drastically different from what they'd known. . . .

We've lost our place in the world, because our presence is no longer needed, and . . . in addition to being unnecessary—or perhaps because of it—we've also become invisible.

Feeling Useless

Where, then, did the idea of "the golden years" come from? Is this just media hype that has no relation to the reality of people's experience in old age? Or was it a more or less apt description of some earlier time? Maybe when people lived only a few years after retirement, the relief from a lifetime of work and tight schedules, the freedom to allow themselves to expand fully into the space they inhabit, to take up activities they never had time for before, did indeed make those years golden. Maybe so many of us feel them so differently now because they last so long. . . .

How do you plan for a future when you don't know when time will stop? That's true for all of us, of course, but for the old it has an immediacy that can't be denied. It's not just the realization that we're close to the end that makes this time so difficult. For the pleasure in our freedom to "just be" comes with the understanding that it's possible only because we've become superfluous, because we've lost our place in the world, because our presence is no longer needed, and that in addition to being unnecessary—or perhaps because of it—we've also become invisible, just another one of the old people, featureless and indistinguishable from one another, who take up space on the bus. . . .

Still, outside the social-sexual arena, even men aren't immune to the invisibility of age, which follows all of us into many corners of life where we used to be seen, whether on the job or in the social world. How can it be otherwise in a society that idolizes youth, that has little reverence for its own history, that moves so quickly that yesterday's knowledge is rendered obsolete today? In such a social setting, whatever wisdom about life we who are old have gathered seems like ancient history, not . . . What's that word that has been so prominent in our national discourse for the last several decades? Ah yes, "relevance." We're not relevant.

As the years pass, many begin to complain that they're living too long, that life no longer has meaning.

"I'm a lot smarter today than I was thirty years ago, and I'm better at my job now than I was then," says a sixty-five-year-old executive who lost his job to one of those corporate mergers we know so well these days. "But these yo-yo kids who are in charge don't even see me and what I can do; they only see my age, and that's the end of it."

A plight common enough to warrant a *New Yorker* cartoon featuring a cigar-smoking, bewildered-looking seventy-something man looking out the window of the office he's about to leave for good and saying ruefully, "I think I've acquired some wisdom over the years, but there doesn't seem to be much demand for it." . . .

What's the Point?

The early retirement years may be pleasurable, may even be wonderful for some. But as the years pass, many begin to complain that they're living too long, that life no longer has meaning.

"What's the point. I can't do all the things I used to do anymore, and I don't even want to," exclaims an eighty-nine-year-old woman. "What? Another trip to someplace I've already been to too many times? Another club meeting? I know before I get there what everyone in my book club is going to say. I'm tired; it's time to lay my head down and go. What are those scientists doing, using all that brainpower to get us to live longer? I want to know, what's the point?"

What's the point? It's not a frivolous question. I ask a mid-sixties friend if she'd like to live to one hundred, and she replies with a grimace, a shudder, and an unequivocal "No."

"Why?" I want to know.

"What would I do for all those years?" she asks.

Giving Up Driving Is Difficult

Anita Creamer

Anita Creamer is a reporter for the Sacramento Bee, *a daily newspaper in Sacramento, California.*

Darlene Snow relishes drivers' friendly waves as she pedals her oversized three-wheeler on the streets of Elk Grove. Three years ago, she voluntarily gave up her driver's license, frightened after she realized how much vision she'd lost in her left eye.

The carless life hasn't been easy for her.

"I've given up smoking and drinking," said Snow, now 76, a retired vocational nurse. "I've given up men. The hardest thing by far was to give up driving. This one's a doozy. It's the lack of your freedom.

"But I ask myself, 'Would you want to hurt someone or have an accident?'"

When is it time for seniors to give up the car keys? The answer varies: As [California] Department of Motor Vehicles senior ombudsman Charley Fenner says, some drivers remain sharp and capable at 90, while others don't belong behind the wheel at 65.

"Basically, our position is that you give it up when you can no longer drive safely," he said.

For families looking for guidance, that's not enough. Answers, though few, are crucial to a rapidly aging society. In two decades' time, one in four American drivers will be 65 or older, up from one in seven now, according to the AARP Public Policy Institute.

With more than 2.5 million drivers 70 and older already on California roads, how do we balance seniors' need for independent lives with public safety concerns?

Christine Craft knows the downside. On March 23, an elderly driver struck Craft and a fellow lawyer, David Belden, as they were walking to lunch on Capitol Avenue.

According to police reports, the 84-year-old woman hit the accelerator instead of the brakes, leaving Belden with a broken leg and Craft with broken ribs, a compression fracture of the spine and a mottled rainbow of what she calls really gnarly bruises.

Losing a license isn't just a transportation issue. The inability to continue driving can be a tipping point, leading to a deepening spiral of isolation and depression.

"I'm a little too old to do a somersault off the hood of an Acura going full speed," said Craft, 65, the radio broadcaster and former TV anchor. "You hear the squealing tires and the engine racing. She hit the accelerator full bore."

Loss of Independence

For the elderly, losing a license isn't just a transportation issue. The inability to continue driving can be a tipping point, leading to a deepening spiral of isolation and depression.

"Put yourself in their shoes," said Therese Schultz, executive director of Senior Center of Elk Grove. "Driving is a sign of independence. It's difficult to surrender. Very few people actually say it's time."

They may not have a choice.

California already requires drivers 70 and older to take the written licensing test and have their eyes examined every five years. To compel a driving test, a doctor's formal report is required. A traffic ticket will also do the trick.

In many cases, a serious conversation is all it takes for an older relative to relinquish the keys. If nothing else works, concerned families can also report their loved ones to the DMV [Department of Motor Vehicles] for retesting.

Slower reaction time, impaired flexibility and coordination, and vision and hearing loss all can wreak havoc on driving skills.

So can dementia, obviously enough, although a recent American Academy of Neurology report indicates that three-fourths of people with mild cases of dementia can still pass their driving tests.

"It's a huge issue for people with dementia," said Ruth Gay, Northern California public policy director for the Alzheimer's Association. "As people develop dementia, they lose the reasoning and judgment to decide whether they're doing a good job with driving."

When dementia increases, California mandates that doctors report that finding to the health department, which forwards it to the DMV.

Even so, Geri Hyman, 78, who lives at Sun City Roseville, said: "A lot of people tell me their husbands with Alzheimer's disease are still driving."

She was able to avoid that alarming prospect with her husband, Hank, 81, whose Alzheimer's worsened a year ago.

"I told him last summer it was time for him to stop driving," she said. "He loved driving. He said no. I said, 'God forbid you hit somebody, they'll sue us.' I had my son come with his family to visit us. When they left, they took the car.

"My husband was in a tizzy when he saw the car was gone. For three months, he'd open the garage door every day when he got up."

Beyond financial liability, elderly drivers reluctant to relinquish the car keys face a deeper question: Do you want to go to your grave having injured or killed someone?

Darlene Snow didn't.

"Every time I hear sirens on Elk Grove Boulevard, I think, 'That could be me,'" she said. "My intellect prevails. I don't belong on the road anymore.

"But I still wash my Lexus every couple of days. I gave up a lot when I gave up (driving) that car."

Isolation in Old Age Is Depressing, Especially for Immigrants

Paul Kleyman

Paul Kleyman writes for New America Media, a national collaboration of ethnic news organizations.

It's not surprising that Robert Lyons slipped into depression a few years ago, except that he was among the growing number of elders living alone, who were lucky enough to get the help he needed to pull him out of his deep funk.

The usually upbeat Lyons, 78, watched his parents and all of his siblings—eight of them—die within a few short years. He also lost most of his friends in his circle of army buddies, who had moved to San Francisco in the 1940s and '50s, partly to escape Southern segregation.

"It was kind of a dark time for me," said Lyons, recalling his sister's terminal cancer, his two remaining brothers' losing struggles with diabetes, and his own health challenges—lingering effects of a stroke in 1993 and, recently, a broken hip. Family trips to his native Texas, surrounded by nieces and nephews, would be a thing of his past.

"So I guess I went off into this depression thing," he said.

Seniors Who Live Alone Face Hardships

Lyons is among the more than one elder in four living alone in the United States, according to a recent report from the Pew Research Center. That's more than double the percentage of Americans of all ages living on their own. The impact of loneliness is even sharper for many immigrant elders, often isolated further by culture and language.

"Adults ages 65 and older who [are] living alone report they are not in as good health and are more likely to feel sad, depressed or lonely than are older adults who live with another person," says the Pew report, released in March [2010].

The Pew researchers found that one-quarter of those living solo reported feeling depressed, versus only one in seven older adults residing with a spouse or other person.

African American seniors, such as Lyons, are especially prone to living by themselves (31.7 percent), according to the Pew study, followed closely by whites. Only one in five Latino elders lives alone.

But Lyons counts himself among the lucky. His senior health program at San Francisco's Institute on Aging provided him access to a psychiatrist, who treated him with antidepressants and talk therapy.

The highest suicide rates are for people 65-plus—and even worse for those 85 or older.

After three years, said Lyons, "It worked because I snapped out of it." He added, "That was a big turnaround for me in my life. I kind of got back on track."

According to the Pew study, "Older folks who live alone enjoy fewer benefits of aging" than seniors who live with someone. Those on their own have less time with family, have fewer interests or hobbies and volunteer less often.

The highest suicide rates are for people 65-plus—and even worse for those 85 or older.

Today, Lyons receives daily calls from the Institute on Aging's Friendship Line, a nationally emulated telephone service for suicide prevention and grief counseling. Program counselors call to chat, gauge his mood and remind him to take his medications or help arrange medical appointments in vans suitable for patients with wheelchairs or walkers. Lyons uses both.

Lyons, like many others, enjoys being independent as they age. A self-described "news junkie," he watches hours of public affairs programs and takes advantage of the monthly activities calendar—listing such things as exercise classes, dances and nature walks—for Fellowship Manor, his low-income senior living apartment building run by the Bethel AME Church.

A lifelong loner who was married briefly in his 30s, Lyons is among only 17.9 percent of older American men living on their own, compared with 34.4 percent of senior women.

Asian Elders Isolated

The challenges of isolation and social exclusion are even more difficult for immigrants.

Psychologist Terry Gock, who directs Asian Pacific Family Center in the San Gabriel Valley section of Los Angeles County, said outreach is critical to locating isolated elders.

Not only is language a major barrier to social interaction, Gock said, "You have an older adult who has never driven in this large space, where houses are far apart, and you cannot walk to practically anywhere in Los Angeles. So they become very housebound."

Noting the growing elder population, the mental health center started its Older Adult Supportive and Integrated Service (OASIS) program two years ago. The staff reached out to find isolated elders through community agencies, senior centers and religious organizations.

Gock dispelled the myth that older Asians have low rates of mental health problems. He stressed that clinical depression among Asian elders is often missed by common screening questions that American medical or counseling professionals ask to identify clinical depression, anxiety or other disorders.

"Even if you ask about being sad or depressed—and it's hard to even ask that in Asian languages—they'd probably say no," Gock explained. But practitioners might well get a different answer if, instead of inquiring whether the older person is sad, translating into Chinese the question, "Does your heart not feel good?"

Similarly, Gock emphasized that providers might elicit a "no" to a question about whether a senior frequently feels angry. "But they can tell you that their liver is on fire. So, the symptoms a service provider asks about can create a very different picture of what symptoms [Asian seniors] have."

Often, Gock said, the stigma of mental illness in Asian communities has delayed elders or family members from seeking help. He continued, "They might have symptoms of psychosis—hearing voices, taking to the wall and sometimes acting uncontrollably. However, the family has been taking care of them for 20 years without medication."

Many elders enjoy the experience of living on their own. But rates of ill health and mental distress are higher among isolated elders.

Ghosts in the Living Room

Anne Wong, who directs the center's OASIS program, recalled a "very special client," a Chinese woman living alone in senior housing, who was referred to the program by the local adult protective services.

The woman was frightened of ghosts she believed were in her living room, so she barricaded herself in her bedroom with a small refrigerator and microwave and used a bucket to urinate.

When Wong and her staff could not coax the woman out of her room, they called a Christian couple the woman had listed as her emergency contact with the housing manager. The couple, who had been bringing the woman food every week or so, finally persuaded the woman to open the door. On finding the woman in filth, they got her to a medical facility where she died soon thereafter.

"It was very sad and exhausting for our staff," said Wong, "but they felt honored to help someone at the end stage of her life."

Wong stressed that community education about treatable mental health conditions is central to the center's work. She has participated in Asian-community radio and other media interviews aimed at destigmatizing mental illness.

Isolated Elders Surrounded by Family with None to Listen

Many elders enjoy the experience of living on their own. But rates of ill health and mental distress are higher among isolated elders, according to a recent report from the Pew Research Center.

For those in emotional pain, no service or intervention is more crucial than one that offers a trained and understanding ear. Older adults can find themselves psychologically isolated in many ways, said Patrick Arbore, founder and director of San Francisco's Friendship Line.

Arbore recalled a Chinese man, who called several years ago to talk about his wish to die. As with many older people in existential distress, this man was not suicidal, but was immersed in thoughts of death—before they think of taking action. That's an important distinction Arbore and his staff make when they first talk with a caller—and the reason he changed the service's name from its original and off-putting Suicide Prevention for the Elderly.

The Chinese man, a retired professional, had lost his wife of 50 years to a series of strokes. Although he said he and his wife had never believed in religion, he began to imagine that her soul was caught in a kind of limbo without him and needed him to join her to lead her to their rest.

"My wife doesn't know where to go," he told Arbore. "She was everything to me."

Although the man had family in the area, his two adult children—both doctors—were always too busy with their active lives and family. When he tried bringing up his feelings, they missed the point by reassuring him that he'd get over his grief eventually.

"It's the worst thing to be old and feel alone in the world."

Arbore explained, "He needed to talk about his relationship with his wife."

Unlike suicide prevention lines, which focus on intervention and discourage chronic callers, Arbore designed the Friendship Line to encourage long talks and multiple calls with staff trained in active listening.

Whether elders phone in or are referred by a mental health professional, the staff will follow up and call daily to chat and help distressed seniors make it through another day.

"Old people need to be listened to," Arbore said, "to be heard and talked to. It's the worst thing to be old and feel alone in the world."

Elderly Same-Sex Couples May Lose Their Right to Make Choices

Joe Mirabella

Joe Mirabella is a professional content producer for an online re-tailer and a featured blogger for several organizations.

There is nothing more personal than how we wish to spend our final years. After decades with our loved ones, there should be no dispute that we should get to spend our final moments together. Unfortunately Sonoma County, CA, treated Harold and Clay as if they were strangers.

Harold was 88 and Clay was 77 when their 20-year relationship was assaulted by Sonoma County. Harold's time here was coming to an end. He was ill and life was further complicated when he took a tumble down the stairs of their home. Harold was taken to the hospital.

Like most same-sex couples who are committed to taking care of each other in sickness and in health, Harold and Clay set up legal documents prior to their personal crisis that were supposed to tell authorities to honor their relationship. Clay should have been able to visit Harold in the hospital and make decisions about his care. Instead, the county and health care professionals refused to let Clay even visit Harold in the hospital.

Tragic as that was, the county was not done with this family. More brutality than any government should inflict on a family—they separated Clay and Harold by placing them in different nursing homes. Remember, Clay was in good health. He was involuntarily committed.

Rights Were Violated

Kate Kendell, the national director for the National Center for Lesbian Rights, a national legal organization committed to advancing the legal and human rights of lesbian, gay, bisexual, and transgender [LGBT] people wrote for the Bilerico Project [an LGBT blog]:

> Ignoring Clay's significant role in Harold's life, the county continued to treat Harold like he had no family and went to court seeking the power to make financial decisions on his behalf. Outrageously, the county represented to the judge that Clay was merely Harold's "roommate." The court denied their efforts, but did grant the county limited access to one of Harold's bank accounts to pay for his care.

After decades with our loved ones, there should be no dispute that we should get to spend our final moments together.

What happened next is even more chilling.

Without authority, without determining the value of Clay and Harold's possessions accumulated over the course of their 20 years together or making any effort to determine which items belonged to whom, the county took everything Harold and Clay owned and auctioned off all of their belongings. Adding further insult to grave injury, the county removed Clay from his home and confined him to a nursing home against his will. The county workers then terminated Clay and Harold's lease and surrendered the home they had shared for many years to the landlord.

Three months after he was hospitalized, Harold died in the nursing home. Because of the county's actions, Clay missed the final months he should have had with his partner of 20 years. Compounding this tragedy, Clay has literally nothing left of the home he had shared with Harold or the life he was living up until the day that Harold fell, because he has been unable to recover any of his property. The only memento Clay has is a photo album that Harold painstakingly put together for Clay during the last three months of his life.

Clay was eventually released from the nursing home following a lawsuit. A further lawsuit is pending [as of April 18, 2010] against Sonoma County, the auction company, and the nursing home.

As important as this lawsuit is, there is nothing any government, court, or lawyer can do to return the dignity and respect Harold and Clay were deprived. No authority will be able to return the last few months of Harold's life, or the chance for Clay and Harold to embrace each other one last time.

We need full legal recognition for same-sex couples—in name and law—in every state in this country. We need it now.

[*Editor's note: A few days before the lawsuit was to go to trial, Sonoma County settled out of court, admitting no misconduct but agreeing to pay Clay Greene and the estate of Harold Scull more than $650,000.*]

Growing Old Is Not as Unpleasant as Younger Adults Expect It to Be

Paul Taylor

Paul Taylor is the executive vice president of the Pew Research Center, a nonpartisan think tank, and director of its Social & Demographic Trends project.

Getting old isn't nearly as bad as people think it will be. Nor is it quite as good.

On aspects of everyday life ranging from mental acuity to physical dexterity to sexual activity to financial security, a new [2009] Pew Research Center Social & Demographic Trends survey on aging among a nationally representative sample of 2,969 adults finds a sizable gap between the expectations that young and middle-aged adults have about old age and the actual experiences reported by older Americans themselves.

These disparities come into sharpest focus when survey respondents are asked about a series of negative benchmarks often associated with aging, such as illness, memory loss, an inability to drive, an end to sexual activity, a struggle with loneliness and depression, and difficulty paying bills. In every instance, older adults report experiencing them at lower levels (often far lower) than younger adults report expecting to encounter them when they grow old.

At the same time, however, older adults report experiencing fewer of the benefits of aging that younger adults expect to enjoy when they grow old, such as spending more time with their family, traveling more for pleasure, having more time for hobbies, doing volunteer work or starting a second career.

These generation gaps in perception also extend to the most basic question of all about old age: When does it begin? Survey respondents ages 18 to 29 believe that the average person becomes old at age 60. Middle-aged respondents put the threshold closer to 70, and respondents ages 65 and above say that the average person does not become old until turning 74.

Other potential markers of old age—such as forgetfulness, retirement, becoming sexually inactive, experiencing bladder control problems, getting gray hair, having grandchildren—are the subjects of similar perceptual gaps. For example, nearly two-thirds of adults ages 18 to 29 believe that when someone "frequently forgets familiar names," that person is old. Less than half of all adults ages 30 and older agree.

The older people get, the younger they feel—relatively speaking.

However, a handful of potential markers—failing health, an inability to live independently, an inability to drive, difficulty with stairs—engender agreement across all generations about the degree to which they serve as an indicator of old age.

Grow Older, Feel Younger

The survey findings would seem to confirm the old saw that you're never too old to feel young. In fact, it shows that *the older people get, the younger they feel*—relatively speaking. Among 18- to 29-year-olds, about half say they feel their age, while about a quarter say they feel older than their age and another quarter say they feel younger. By contrast, among adults 65 and older, fully 60% say they feel younger than their age, compared with 32% who say they feel exactly their age and just 3% who say they feel older than their age.

Moreover, the gap in years between actual age and "felt age" widens as people grow older. Nearly half of all survey respondents ages 50 and older say they feel at least 10 years younger than their chronological age. Among respondents ages 65 to 74, a third say they feel 10 to 19 years younger than their age, and one in six say they feel at least 20 years younger than their actual age.

In sync with this upbeat way of counting their felt age, older adults also have a count-my-blessings attitude when asked to look back over the full arc of their lives. Nearly half (45%) of adults ages 75 and older say their life has turned out better than they expected, while just 5% say it has turned out worse (the remainder say things have turned out the way they expected or have no opinion). All other age groups also tilt positive, but considerably less so, when asked to assess their lives so far against their own expectations.

Nearly half (45%) of adults ages 75 and older say their life has turned out better than they expected.

The Downside of Getting Old

To be sure, there *are* burdens that come with old age. About one in four adults ages 65 and older report experiencing memory loss. About one in five say they have a serious illness, are not sexually active, or often feel sad or depressed. About one in six report they are lonely or have trouble paying bills. One in seven cannot drive. One in ten say they feel they aren't needed or are a burden to others.

But when it comes to these and other potential problems related to old age, the share of younger and middle-aged adults who report expecting to encounter them is much higher than the share of older adults who report actually experiencing them.

Moreover, these problems are not equally shared by all groups of older adults. Those with low incomes are more likely than those with high incomes to face these challenges.

The only exception to this pattern has to do with sexual inactivity; the likelihood of older adults reporting a problem in this realm of life is not correlated with income.

The vast majority of the "old old" in our survey appear to have made peace with their circumstances.

Not surprisingly, troubles associated with aging accelerate as adults advance into their 80s and beyond. For example, about four in ten respondents (41%) ages 85 and older say they are experiencing some memory loss, compared with 27% of those ages 75–84 and 20% of those ages 65–74. Similarly, 30% of those ages 85 and older say they often feel sad or depressed, compared with less than 20% of those who are 65–84. And a quarter of adults ages 85 and older say they no longer drive, compared with 17% of those ages 75–84 and 10% of those who are 65–74.

But even in the face of these challenges, the vast majority of the "old old" in our survey appear to have made peace with their circumstances. Only a miniscule share of adults ages 85 and older—1%—say their lives have turned out worse than they expected. It no doubt helps that adults in their late 80s are as likely as those in their 60s and 70s to say that they are experiencing many of the good things associated with aging—be it time with family, less stress, more respect or more financial security.

The Upside of Getting Old

When asked about a wide range of potential benefits of old age, seven in ten respondents ages 65 and older say they are enjoying more time with their family. About two-thirds cite more time for hobbies, more financial security and not having to work. About six in ten say they get more respect and feel less stress than when they were younger. Just over half cite more time to travel and to do volunteer work. . . . Older adults may not be experiencing these "upsides" at quite the prevalence levels that most younger adults expect to enjoy them once they grow old, but their responses nonetheless indicate that the phrase "golden years" is something more than a syrupy greeting card sentiment.

Of all the good things about getting old, the best by far, according to older adults, is being able to spend more time with family members. In response to an open-ended question, 28% of those ages 65 and older say that what they value most about being older is the chance to spend more time with family, and an additional 25% say that above all, they value time with their grandchildren. A distant third on this list is having more financial security, which was cited by 14% of older adults as what they value most about getting older.

People Are Living Longer

These survey findings come at a time when older adults account for record shares of the populations of the United States and most developed countries. Some 39 million Americans, or 13% of the U.S. population, are 65 and older—up from 4% in 1900. The century-long expansion in the share of the world's population that is 65 and older is the product of dramatic advances in medical science and public health as well as steep declines in fertility rates. In this country, the increase has leveled off since 1990, but it will start rising again when the first wave of the nation's 76 million baby boomers turn 65 in 2011. By 2050, according to Pew Research projections, about one in five Americans will be over age 65, and about 5% will be ages 85 and older, up from 2% now. These ratios will put the U.S. at mid-century roughly where Japan, Italy and Germany—the three "oldest" large countries in the world—are today.

Contacting Older Adults

Any survey that focuses on older adults confronts one obvious methodological challenge: A small but not insignificant share of people 65 and older are either too ill or incapacitated to take part in a 20-minute telephone survey, or they live in an institutional setting such as a nursing home where they cannot be contacted.

We assume that the older adults we were unable to reach for these reasons have a lower quality of life, on average, than those we did reach. To mitigate this problem, the survey included interviews with more than 800 adults whose parents are ages 65 or older. We asked these adult children many of the same questions about their parents' lives that we asked of older adults about their own lives. These "surrogate" respondents provide a window on the experiences of the full population of older adults, including those we could not reach directly. Not surprisingly, the portrait of old age they draw is somewhat more negative than the one painted by older adult respondents themselves. . . .

Perceptions About Aging

The Generation Gap, Circa 2009. In a 1969 Gallup poll, 74% of respondents said there was a generation gap, with the phrase defined in the survey question as "a major difference in the point of view of younger people and older people today." When the same question was asked a decade later, in 1979, by CBS and the *New York Times*, just 60% perceived a generation gap. But in perhaps the single-most intriguing finding in this new Pew Research survey, the share that say there is a generation gap has spiked to 79%—despite the fact that there have been few overt generational conflicts in recent times of the sort that roiled the 1960s. It could be that the phrase now means something different, and less confrontational, than it did at the height of the counterculture's defiant challenges to the establishment 40 years ago. Whatever the current understanding of the term "generation gap," roughly equal shares of young, middle-aged and older respondents in the new survey agree that such a gap exists. The most common explanation offered by respondents of all ages has to do with differences in morality, values and work ethic. Relatively few cite differences in political outlook or in uses of technology.

When Does Old Age Begin? At 68. That's the average of all answers from the 2,969 survey respondents. But as noted above, this average masks a wide, age-driven variance in responses. More than half of adults under 30 say the average person becomes old even before turning 60. Just 6% of adults who are 65 or older agree. Moreover, gender as well as age influences attitudes on this subject. Women, on average, say a person becomes old at age 70. Men, on average, put the number at 66. In addition, on all 10 of the nonchronological potential markers of old age tested in this survey, men are more inclined than women to say the marker is a proxy for old age.

Are You Old? Certainly not! Public opinion in the aggregate may decree that the average person becomes old at age 68, but you won't get too far trying to convince people that age that the threshold applies to them. Among respondents ages 65–74, just 21% say they feel old. Even among those who are 75 and older, just 35% say they feel old.

The same factors that predict happiness among younger adults—good health, good friends and financial security—by and large predict happiness among older adults.

[To] What Age Would You Like to Live? The average response from our survey respondents is 89. One in five would like to live into their 90s, and 8% say they'd like to surpass the century mark. The public's verdict on the most desirable life span appears to have ratcheted down a bit in recent years. A 2002 AARP [an advocacy organization for older Americans] survey found that the average desired life span was 92.

Everyday Life

What Do Older People Do Every Day? Among all adults ages 65 and older, nine in ten talk with family or friends every day.

About eight in ten read a book, newspaper or magazine, and the same share takes a prescription drug daily. Three-quarters watch more than an hour of television; about the same share prays daily. Nearly two-thirds drive a car. Less than half spend time on a hobby. About four in ten take a nap; about the same share goes shopping. Roughly one in four uses the Internet, gets vigorous exercise or has trouble sleeping. Just 4% get into an argument with someone. As adults move deeper into their 70s and 80s, daily activity levels diminish on most fronts—especially when it comes to exercising and driving. On the other hand, daily prayer and daily medication both increase with age.

Are Older Adults Happy? They're about as happy as everyone else. And perhaps more importantly, the same factors that predict happiness among younger adults—good health, good friends and financial security—by and large predict happiness among older adults. However, there are a few age-related differences in life's happiness sweepstakes. Most notably, once all other key demographic variables are held constant, being married is a predictor of happiness among younger adults but not among older adults (perhaps because a significant share of the latter group is made up of widows or widowers, many of whom presumably have "banked" some of the key marriage-related correlates of happiness, such as financial security and a strong family life). Among all older adults, happiness varies very little by age, gender or race.

Some Elderly People Enjoy Their Old Age

Jerry Large

Jerry Large is a staff columnist for the Seattle Times.

Eileen Allen likes herself. That is a huge thing, and if you knew her you'd like her, too.

She's 91 and she told me, "This time of my life is the best time of my life. I've finally gotten to know me."

She has no illusions about aging. Allen has lost most of her vision and hearing. She needs a walker or cane to get around. She watched her husband of 54 years die of cancer.

But Allen has chosen to be happy, and she wants other people to know they can make that choice.

A friend of hers called to tell me Allen has written and published a book about just that, *I Like Being Old: A Guide to Making the Most of Aging.*

In overcoming and adapting to the challenges of old age, she has learned that Eileen Allen is OK. "I've discovered I can do things I wouldn't have dreamed I could do." She thinks other people might like to know how to do that, too.

A good life doesn't just happen, she said: "Happiness is an inside job."

Writing has always been one of her pleasures, but Allen couldn't write this book alone because she can't see the words. She enlisted the help of a friend, Judith Starbuck, a journalist Allen met when they both worked as editors on the newsletter of the Crone of Puget Sound—"Women growing old with power, passion and purpose."

Starbuck, who is only 68, took down Allen's words and did the editing Allen could no longer do herself. They've become fast friends.

Allen has chosen to be happy, and she wants other people to know they can make that choice.

Allen writes about moving from a brick Tudor, to a condo after her husband's death, then to a retirement community, shedding more of her stuff with each move. About leaning on friends, but not too much. She writes about giving up her car and realizing cooking was too dangerous.

New Enjoyment of Simple Things

Each time she had to learn to compensate, and sometimes she found a new enjoyment of simple things. She writes that when she could no longer tend plants, she watched nature take over her garden. Rather than resting, she felt happy to be embraced by nature. Trading a long to-do list for time spent reflecting, or enjoying the dance of a small bird, isn't a loss.

She lives at the Hearthstone [a senior community] now and takes great pleasure in walking the nearly three miles around Green Lake. She couldn't get around the lake without her walker, but for the longest time she resisted getting one. She didn't want the stigma, until a bad fall changed her mind.

Then she had to overcome her worry that she couldn't walk very far. She did it methodically, by walking a few feet, counting her steps, then adding more steps each week, until she could make it all the way around.

Allen calls her walker, "the biggest emancipation I have given myself."

She stands up straight and looks ahead when she uses hers. She is purposeful about approaching old age.

Allen started thinking about aging when she turned 60. She watched how different people handled it. She writes that she saw grumpies with sour faces and lots of complaints; coasters, just letting life do with them whatever it would. And there were seekers, always adapting and shaping their lives in response to changing circumstances. That's the group she chose to join.

"God knows when you get old there is enough to be unhappy about," but what is the use, she asks, of sitting and stewing? People are living longer and it would be a tragedy to waste those extra years, she said, so why not learn to make the most of them?

That philosophy goes beyond aging.

Allen was for years a professor and researcher in child development. Much focus was on helping children with developmental disabilities reach new skill levels. She told me about a boy who'd never dressed himself, and she beamed with joy describing the first time he pulled on a sock.

Her philosophy then was start where you are and move forward. That's what she is doing now, but she didn't always apply that idea to herself. She was 34 and a mother of three when she took her first college class, and she only did it because a friend nudged her into it. What if she hadn't tried?

"I was raised with constant criticism," she said. Self-doubt has been a constant for her. Taking control of her aging has helped silence those doubts.

Allen doesn't shrink from trying now, and it is this new version of herself she likes so much.

I think she is delightful, too.

Old Age Can Bring Serenity, and in Some Cases, New Achievements

Jeanne Conte

Jeanne Conte is an author based in Ohio.

> "Grow old along with me; the best is yet to be, the last of life, for which the first was made."—Robert Browning

> "Gray hair is a crown of glory; it is gained by virtuous Living."—Proverbs 16:31

I was sure this was the rationalization of someone over the hill when I first encountered these words as a young student of English literature. However, Robert Browning's tribute to age in his poem "Rabbi Ben Ezra" intrigued me enough to be remembered into the latter days of my life. And, on reflection, I see his wisdom.

Robert Browning actually wrote these words when he was 52 years old and a widower, three years after the death of his beloved wife, Elizabeth [Barrett] Browning. Perhaps he was dreaming . . . wishful thinking, because he had so deeply loved his wife. Literary experts believe that the meaning of the poem was that a person is not to be measured by his or her work capabilities, but by character molded by time and life.

Throughout my life, when asked about beauty, I always seemed to startle my interrogators by stating that the most beautiful woman I'd ever seen was my grandmother. She had a soft, lilac beauty about her. Her face always wore a smile, crowned by silver hair waved gently to a bun atop her head. She carried herself with dignity, yet warmed to my needs and those of others. Her contented life with my grandfather reflected perfectly, "Grow old along with me; the best is yet to be. . . ."

Youth is so encumbered with stress—pressures of education and then of acquisition and career. With well over 50 percent of marriages failing, add the strain of relationships. Conversely, I do not mean to minimize acute problems of age—health, difficult monetary position and loss of loved ones. I only notice that I find my latter years and those of many others somewhat more comfortable, often more productive and frequently more enriched.

Golden Achievements

Many examples are available of the capabilities of those in their later years. [Pierre-Simon] Laplace worked on his astronomy until he passed on at 70, crying, "What we know is nothing; what we do not know is immense!" John Milton wrote the 10-volume *Paradise Lost* at age 57, 13 years after becoming totally blind. Ludwig van Beethoven composed his Ninth Symphony after he became deaf in the fifth decade of his life.

I find my latter years and those of many others somewhat more comfortable, often more productive and frequently more enriched.

Grandma [Anna Mary Robertson] Moses began painting when most people retire. [Prussian/German statesman Otto von] Bismarck did his greatest work after he was 70.

My own mother, in the eighth decade of her life, established a library and school in Pakistan while there with my father who, also in his 70s, worked as a consulting engineer assisting that developing nation. My husband, in his 80s, conducts his own business.

When there first was legislation proposed in the Ohio legislature that would have allowed life support systems to be discontinued for the elderly in hospitals if the medical personnel deemed their quality of life to be less than worthy of continuation, there were two legislators there who were father and son. The father was very ill in a local hospital where he had been confined for some time. His son refused to support the bill stating that a person's present productivity should never be criteria for whether or not he or she could contribute to the world in other ways, and should never be reason for allowing one to die. The bill went down in resounding defeat.

Peace and Serenity

Now, as I reflect on my own life, I can see how "the last of life" can be that "for which the first was made." As a youth who first heard these words, I had my world ahead of me—health, hope, possibilities—but I was not often deeply happy, content nor serene. I suffered acute sensitivity and had years of difficult strivings ahead of me.

Now, as I walk through the more mature years of life, I find I'm freed from the painful extremes of sensitivity, and that the years of striving have woven themselves into a smoother fabric of harmonious relationships. There is a peaceful serenity, now, under which lies a common denominator of contentment. Certainly, troubles come now, as always, and I foresee many more as age creeps on, but I view them from a different perspective and their relative importance purports less emotional stress. I sit on a cushion of a lifetime of experience, and am buffered by the good memories stored for rainy days.

After all, [Johann Wolfgang von] Goethe wrote *Faust* shortly before his death at 99, and [British statesman William Ewart] Gladstone took up a new language at 70. May Sarton, as she wrote a poem almost every day of her 80th year, noted in her journal: "And where have I been? Through a thicket of ill health into an extraordinary time of happiness and fulfillment, more than I ever dreamed possible."

After making one's way through the labyrinth of youth, with character molded on the anvil of life, it does seem perhaps "the best is yet to be, the last of life for which the first was made."

CHAPTER 3

Should More Medical Care Be Provided to the Elderly?

Chapter Preface

Are the elderly in need of more medical care than they are receiving in today's society? Nearly all those over sixty-five are entitled to Medicare, and many also have supplemental insurance that pays for the portion of their medical expenses that Medicare does not cover. The lack of coverage for long-term custodial care is a serious problem acknowledged by almost everyone, but apart from that, it might seem that the elderly are better off than the large number of younger Americans who have no health insurance.

The issue is more complex than it may appear to be, however, and opinions are sharply divided. Some people argue that there is discrimination against the elderly—that they are not offered all the treatment options for serious illnesses, such as cancer, that younger patients are. Many now also fear that the new health care law enacted by Congress in 2010 will lead to "rationing" of medical care and that because the elderly are generally in poorer health than younger adults and have a shorter time left to benefit from treatment, they will bear the brunt of restricted funding.

Advocates for the elderly also point to the fact that elders need specialized care that is not as widely available as it should be. They can be better treated by geriatricians—physicians who specialize in the care of elderly people—than by specialists in particular diseases, yet because Medicare does not provide adequate compensation for the extra time it takes for a doctor to look at an older person's health problems as a whole rather than treat just one disease, few medical students choose that specialty. Also, elders near death do not often receive palliative care, a form of care that focuses on the prevention and relief of suffering instead of on futile attempts to eliminate disease, as this is a new field of medicine in which few doctors are trained and is not offered everywhere.

Therefore, those concerned about the well-being of elderly individuals commonly feel that more money should be devoted to meeting their medical needs. But there is another side to the question. Some knowledgeable people feel strongly that the problem is not that elders receive too little medical treatment, but that they receive too much. According to this minority view, not only does excessive treatment cost money that could be better spent on more appropriate care, but more importantly, it is extremely harmful to elderly patients. Even if funding were unlimited, they say, older people should not be treated in the same way as younger individuals because it is not to their advantage.

In the first place, older people who do not feel sick are often treated with medication for what are generally considered risk factors, such as high cholesterol, just as younger adults are. But some doctors feel that this is not justifiable. An older person may have a larger risk of getting sick than a younger one, but it may be too late for preventative treatment to make any real difference—or, on the other hand, a person who has already reached old age without getting a particular disease may not have enough time left for it to develop. A drug believed to reduce risk may have been statistically shown to help one person out of seventy-five, for example, but what about the other seventy-four people? If they are given that drug, they will needlessly suffer its side effects for the rest of their lives, at a time when they should be helped to feel as well as possible during their remaining years.

The side effects of medication are not always minor, and they tend to affect older people in worse ways than they do younger individuals. Even in the case of drugs elders need to control illness they already have, overdosing—which can happen because older bodies process drugs differently than younger ones—causes harm. Sometimes symptoms attributed to aging, such as shakiness or mental confusion, are actually the result of overmedication, particularly when many drugs taken for different conditions are combined.

Another problem that is troubling in the eyes of those who oppose excessive care is that elderly people frequently receive futile treatment—treatment that is often painful, yet will not prolong their lives by enough to justify the suffering it involves. Sometimes it will not prolong life at all, but is given merely because many doctors treat specific diseases in standard ways without considering whether it will do a particular person more harm than good. Some investigators feel that one reason for this is that it is profitable for hospitals that are paid well by Medicare for certain procedures. On the other hand, patients or their families often demand that "everything" be done, under the mistaken assumption that treating illness is inherently beneficial.

There are a few medical ethicists who argue that people in their eighties or older should not receive expensive, high-tech medical intervention because it is too costly to society to prolong their lives by a short time after they have already lived a full life. But this is not the most common objection to such intervention. Much more frequent, especially on the part of nurses and others who have had contact with the dying, is the belief that subjecting helpless older people to the full range of medical technology is cruel. Those who favor it, they say, are under the illusion that death can be warded off indefinitely, or at least that medicine should proceed as if that were the aim. In many people's opinion, it would be better if the aged were allowed to die naturally in as much comfort as truly compassionate care can provide.

The Need for Long-Term Care Is Not Being Met

Jane Gross

Jane Gross is the founding blogger of The New Old Age, *one of many blogs maintained by the* New York Times.

Not long ago Dr. Joanne Lynn, a geriatrician who pulls no punches in her frequent critiques of America's sorry system of end-of-life care, looked out from the dais of a Washington, D.C., ballroom at a sea of middle-aged faces: health policy makers, legislative staff, advocates for the aged and for family caregivers—an audience of experts.

"How many of you expect to die?" she asked.

The audience fell silent, laughed nervously and only then, looking one to the other, slowly raised their hands.

"Would you prefer to be old when it happens?" she then asked.

This time the response was swift and sure, given the alternative.

Then Dr. Lynn, who describes herself as an "old person in training," offered three options to the room. Who would choose cancer as the way to go? Just a few. Chronic heart failure, or emphysema? A few more.

"So all the rest of you are up for frailty and dementia?" Dr. Lynn asked.

On the screen above the dais, she showed graphs describing the three most common ways that old people die and the trajectory and duration of each scenario. Cancer deaths, which peak at age 65, usually come after many years of good health followed by a few weeks or months of steep decline, according to Dr. Lynn's data. The 20 percent of Americans who die this way need excellent medical care during the long period of high functioning, she said, and then hospice support for both patient and family during the sprint to death.

Death following extended frailty and dementia is everyone's worst nightmare, an interminable and humiliating series of losses for the patient, and an exhausting and potentially bankrupting ordeal for the family.

Deaths from organ failure, generally heart or lung disease, peak among patients 10 years older, killing about one in four Americans around age 75 after a far bumpier course. These patients' lives are punctuated by bouts of severe illness alternating with periods of relative stability. At some point rescue attempts fail, and then death is sudden. What these patients and families need, Dr. Lynn said, is consistent disease management to head off crises, aggressive intervention at the first hint of trouble and advance planning for how to manage the final emergency.

Everyone's Worst Nightmare

The third option, death following extended frailty and dementia, is everyone's worst nightmare, an interminable and humiliating series of losses for the patient, and an exhausting and potentially bankrupting ordeal for the family. Approximately 40 percent of Americans, generally past age 85, follow this course, said Dr. Lynn, and the percentage will grow with improvements in prevention and treatment of cancer, heart disease and pulmonary disease.

These are the elderly who for years on end must depend on the care of loved ones, usually adult daughters, or the kindness of strangers, the aides who care for them at home or in nursing facilities. This was my mother's fate, and she articulated it with mordant humor: The reward for living past age 85 and avoiding all the killer diseases, she said, is that you get to rot to death instead.

Those suffering from physical frailty, as she was, lose the ability to walk, to dress themselves or to move from bed to wheelchair without a Hoyer lift and the strong backs of aides earning so little that many qualify for food stamps. These patients, often referred to as the old-old, require diapers, spoon-feeding and frequent repositioning in bed to avoid bedsores. Those with dementia, most often Alzheimer's disease, lose short-term memory, fail to recognize loved ones, get lost without constant supervision and eventually forget how to speak and swallow.

What all of these patients need, Dr. Lynn said, is custodial care, which can easily cost $100,000 a year and is not reimbursed by Medicare. The program was created in 1965 when hardly anyone lived this long.

"We're doing this so badly because we've never been here before," Dr. Lynn said. "But the care system we've got didn't come down from the mountain. We made it up, and we can make it up better."

Government Control Will Lead to Rationing of Medical Treatment for the Elderly

Wall Street Journal Online

The Wall Street Journal Online *is an Internet version of the popular English-language international daily newspaper.*

Elderly Americans are turning out in droves to fight ObamaCare [the health care bill passed in March 2010], and President [Barack] Obama is arguing back that they have nothing to worry about. Allow us to referee. While claims about euthanasia and "death panels" are over the top, senior fears have exposed a fundamental truth about what Mr. Obama is proposing: Namely, once health care is nationalized, or mostly nationalized, rationing care is inevitable, and those who have lived the longest will find their care the most restricted.

Far from being a scare tactic, this is a logical conclusion based on experience and common sense. Once health care is a "free good" that government pays for, demand will soar and government costs will soar too. When the public finally reaches its taxing limit, something will have to give on the care and spending side. In a word, care will be rationed by politics.

Mr. Obama's reply is that private insurance companies already ration, by deciding which treatments are covered and which aren't. However, there's an ocean of difference between coverage decisions made under millions of voluntary private contracts and rationing via government. An Atlantic Ocean, in fact. Virtually every European government with "universal" health care restricts access in one way or another to control costs, and it isn't pretty.

Rationing Health Care

The British system is most restrictive, using a black-box actuarial formula known as "quality-adjusted life years," or QALYs, that determines who can receive what care. If a treatment isn't deemed to be cost effective for specific populations, particularly the elderly, the National Health Service [NHS] simply doesn't pay for it. Even France—which has a mix of public and private medicine—has fixed reimbursement rates since the 1970s and strictly controls the use of specialists and the introduction of new medical technologies such as CT [computerized tomography] scans and MRIs [magnetic resonance imaging].

Once health care is nationalized, or mostly nationalized, rationing care is inevitable, and those who have lived the longest will find their care the most restricted.

Yes, the U.S. "rations" by ability to pay (though in the end no one is denied actual care). This is true of every good or service in a free economy and a world of finite resources but infinite wants. Yet no one would say we "ration" houses or gasoline because those goods are allocated by prices. The problem is that governments ration through brute force— either explicitly restricting the use of medicine or lowering payments below market rates. Both methods lead to waiting lines, lower quality, or less innovation—and usually all three.

A lot of talk has centered on what [former vice presidential candidate] Sarah Palin inelegantly called "death panels." Of course rationing to save the federal fisc will be subtler than a bureaucratic decision to "pull the plug on grandma," as Mr.

Obama put it. But Mrs. Palin has also exposed a basic truth. A substantial portion of Medicare spending is incurred in the last six months of life.

From the point of view of politicians with a limited budget, is it worth spending a lot on, say, a patient with late-stage cancer where the odds of remission are long? Or should they spend to improve quality, not length, of life? Or pay for a hip or knee replacement for seniors, when palliative care might cost less? And who decides?

In Britain, the NHS decides, and under its QALYs metric it generally won't pay more than $22,000 for treatments to extend a life six months. "Money for the NHS isn't limitless," as one NHS official recently [as of August 2009] put it in response to American criticism, "so we need to make sure the money we have goes on things which offer more than the care we'll have to forgo to pay for them."

Before he got defensive, Mr. Obama was open about this political calculation. He often invokes the experience of his own grandmother, musing whether it was wise for her to receive a hip replacement after a terminal cancer diagnosis. In an April [2009] interview with the New York Times, he wondered whether this represented a "sustainable model" for society. He seems to believe these medical issues are all justifiably *political* questions that government or some panel of philosopher kings can and should decide. No wonder so many seniors rebel at such judgments that they know they could do little to influence, much less change.

Restraining the Growth of Medicare

Mr. Obama has also said many times that the growth of Medicare spending must be restrained, and his budget director Peter Orszag has made it nearly his life's cause. We agree, but then why does Mr. Obama want to add to our fiscal burdens a new Medicare-like program for everyone under 65 too? Medicare already rations care, refusing, for example, to pay for virtual colonoscopies and has payment policies or directives to curtail the use of certain cancer drugs, diagnostic tools, asthma medications and many others. Seniors routinely buy supplemental insurance (Medigap) to patch Medicare's holes—and Medicare is still growing by 11% this year.

The political and fiscal pressure to further ration Medicare would increase exponentially if government is paying for most everyone's care. The better way to slow the growth of Medicare is to give seniors more control over their own health care and the incentives to spend wisely, by offering competitive insurance plans. But this would mean less control for government, not more.

It's striking that even the AARP [an advocacy organization for older Americans]—which is run by liberals who favor national health care—has been backing away from support for Mr. Obama's version. The AARP leadership's Democratic sympathies will probably prevail in the end, perhaps after some price-control sweeteners are added for prescription drugs. But AARP is out of touch with its own members, who have figured out that their own health and lives are at stake in this debate over ObamaCare. They know that when medical discretion clashes with limited government budgets, medicine loses.

The Field of Geriatric Medicine Is Vanishing Because of Inadequate Funding

Lewis A. Lipsitz

Lewis A. Lipsitz is a professor of medicine at Harvard Medical School and codirector of the Institute for Aging Research at Hebrew SeniorLife.

One thing that is lost in the health care debate is how to care for the elderly. It's ironic that at a time when thousands of Americans are struggling to find appropriate care for their failing parents [in 2009], the field of geriatric medicine appears to be vanishing.

For geriatricians, one distinguishing feature of the specialty—and one that most threatens its future—is the in-depth conversations about care between doctors, their older patients, and their families. Critical issues covered include treatment options, the efficacy of treatments, and the impact of these treatments on quality of life. It takes time to manage multiple interacting medical, social, and psychological problems, weigh the risks and benefits of various interventions, and discuss goals of care with patients and their families.

The problem is that geriatricians are not adequately compensated for the time they take to address their patients' complex medical, psychological, and social needs. Consequently, the specialty is not attracting enough physicians to care for our rapidly expanding elderly population. In 2008 there were 7,128 certified geriatricians in the United States. By 2030, we will need 36,000 geriatricians. But the number of graduating physicians seeking specialty training in geriatrics is going in the wrong direction, dropping from 167 in 2003 to 91 in

2007. Fewer doctors are specializing in geriatrics, in part because it does not provide sufficient income to pay off their loans or compensate them fairly for the labor-intensive work.

Looking at the Patient as a Whole

Geriatric medicine cuts across all diseases that contribute to the functional problems an older adult might have. An older patient typically goes from one specialist to another, with each doctor treating a single problem, but often not looking at the patient as a whole. The patient may receive treatment, but quality-of-life goals are rarely discussed.

It is critical to the future health of Americans that the field of geriatric medicine not be allowed to die.

In contrast, the geriatrician often sits with three (or more) individuals: the patient, the patient's spouse, and an adult child. Together they present a medical history and, often, a list of medications prescribed by different doctors. Medicare pays the geriatrician a small fraction of the true cost spent with the patient, taking a history, examining the patient, ordering appropriate tests, making a diagnosis, and developing a treatment plan. Following the visit, the geriatrician reviews laboratory studies, talks to family members and other doctors, organizes rehabilitative and social services, completes applications for supportive housing, renews medications . . . and gets paid nothing for this work.

Ironically, geriatricians actually save health care dollars by planning ahead; avoiding unnecessary hospitalizations, tests, medications, and treatments; reducing hospitalization and surgical complications; shortening lengths of stay; and facilitating the safe transfer of patients to appropriate rehabilitation settings and care at home. President [Barack] Obama's health care bill [passed in March 2010] would, at least, require

Medicare to cover counseling sessions so that physicians can develop appropriate care plans with their elderly patients.

It is critical to the future health of Americans that the field of geriatric medicine not be allowed to die. A first step might be for Congress to tone down the partisan rhetoric and present a more thoughtful discussion about reforming care, not just payment for that care. A second step would be to train medical students so that every emerging doctor has basic knowledge of geriatrics—the way every medical doctor has a working knowledge of cardiology. A third would be to train the academic leaders to teach students about the special issues confronting older patients.

As America's population ages, more people will need to seek the expertise of qualified geriatricians. The health care system must support appropriate, proactive, cost-effective geriatric care in all settings—and help guarantee a healthy future for us all.

The Elderly Are Being Harmed by Overmedication

Margaret Cruikshank

Margaret Cruikshank is a lecturer in women's studies and faculty associate of the Center on Aging at the University of Maine.

Each year, 100,000 Americans or more die of adverse drug reactions, one million are severely injured, and two million are harmed while they are hospitalized, making ill effects from drugs one of the greatest dangers in modern society and one of the leading causes of death, according to Thomas J. Moore, an authority on prescription drugs. The incidence of adverse drug reactions is estimated to be twice to three times greater among the elderly. For them, the physiologic response to drugs is much more scattered and the predictability of drug action is much less certain than in younger people. Approximately 17 percent of hospital admissions of people over seventy are caused by adverse reactions to drugs. Not all of these reactions are caused by overmedication, but gerontologists surmise that it is the most common cause. Forty percent of the respondents to a survey by AARP [an advocacy organization for older Americans] reported side effects from their medications. Overprescribing psychotropic (mood-altering) drugs is a leading cause of adverse reactions. Cough suppressants can cause drowsiness, unsteadiness, and constipation in the old. Prolonged use of antacids causes constipation and can weaken bones. Analgesics [painkillers] containing codeine can cause dizziness and fatigue and increase the effect of most other drugs. Other common reactions to overmedication include impaired movements, memory loss, confusion, anxiety, palpitations, restlessness, insomnia, blocked thyroid function, mood swings or other emotional imbalances, blurred vision, urinary retention, potassium depletion, gastrointestinal pain or bleeding, involuntary movements of the arms and legs, and lessening capacity to smell and taste.

In addition, overuse of drugs can cause nutritional depletion resulting in such problems as hearing loss, anemia, breathlessness, and weakness. Among nutrients lost are vitamins A and C and beta-carotene, all thought likely to help immune systems ward off cancer. Drugs that should not be prescribed for people over sixty-five include some tranquilizers and sedatives, antidepressants, arthritis drugs, pain relievers, dementia treatments, blood thinners, and muscle relaxants. Depression as a side effect of drugs is not limited to tranquilizers and other mood-altering medications. Anti-inflammatory drugs, medications for high blood pressure and high cholesterol, antihistamines, and antibiotics may all cause depression. Milder forms of depression are easily dismissed as natural to aging. Old women are especially at risk for having treatable symptoms attributed to aging itself.

Unrecognized drug interactions can lead to a false diagnosis of Alzheimer's disease.

Alcohol and tobacco interact with prescription drugs, increasing risk factors for elderly people who take multiple drugs. Some arthritis medicines, for example, interact with coffee and alcohol to damage the lining of the stomach. When sleeping pills mix with alcohol, breathing can be impaired to a dangerous degree. Many people over sixty-five use both alcohol and prescription drugs. Concurrent use of these two substances even ten or more hours apart can make drugs much more toxic.

Impaired Mental Function

Unrecognized drug interactions can lead to a false diagnosis of Alzheimer's disease. Although the extent of this problem is hard to determine, it is likely to increase as the aging population increases. Mental function can be impaired by both prescription drugs and over-the-counter medications: steroids such as prednisone, drugs used to treat heart problems and high blood pressure, drugs prescribed for stomach ailments, psychiatric drugs, Parkinson's [disease] drugs, and treatments for anxiety and insomnia.

Of all the adverse consequences of drugs, the effect on cell division is probably the danger most underestimated, according to Thomas J. Moore. It does not show up in routine tests of new drugs, and it may result in large numbers of bone marrow injuries. When cell birth and death are disrupted, cancer, birth defects, and blood disorders may result. Drug catastrophes are not dramatic like plane crashes but tend rather to be "slow, insidious, and difficult to see." Studies of potentially dangerous drugs that should not have been prescribed for the elderly are summarized by Moore. In a nationwide sample of more than six thousand people, 23 percent received drugs that were inappropriate. Using Medicare data, the General Accounting Office [currently known as the Government Accountability Office] found that 17 percent of the drugs prescribed for the old were the wrong ones. These figures probably only hint at the risks run by those over sixty-five who use prescription drugs. Unforeseen side effects not apparent during testing come to light only after the drug is in widespread use, and even more alarming, deaths and injuries from drugs are "vastly underreported." Since old people use so many drugs, they suffer disproportionately from unforeseen side effects and the underreporting of deaths and injuries. For them, a wise precaution would be to avoid any drug on the market for less than a year.

Are women more at risk than men? They appear to metabolize some drugs differently, especially psychotropic ones. A report by the National Center on Addiction and [Substance] Abuse at Columbia University (CASA) states that women over fifty-nine get addicted to alcohol and prescription drugs faster and on smaller amounts than other people, that women are much more likely than men to be given a prescription for a tranquilizer by their physician, and that the use of sedatives and sedating antidepressants doubles the risk of falls and fractures among older women. For either sex, taking more than four prescription drugs is strongly associated with increased fall rates. Common sense suggests that women's smaller body size and hormone changes mean that standard doses of medications are too high, but the susceptibility of older women to side effects has not been studied. "Either no one thinks it's important, or if they do, they don't have funding," according to Katherine Sherif. It would be useful to know, for example, if drug prescribing should take hormone replacement therapy into account. Dr. Sherif points out that the FDA [Food and Drug Administration] now requires that women be included in clinical trials but does not require that study results be broken down by gender. Particularly frustrating is the fact that women must be included only if there is evidence of gender difference, but the evidence comes from research.

Serious Problems in Nursing Homes

Although adverse drug reactions affect the old who live independently or with families as well as those who are institutionalized, the problem is especially serious among nursing home residents. Since this population is largely female, the problem of overmedicating nursing home residents is a women's issue. Some drugs have very similar names, resulting in mix-ups. Many falls in nursing homes result from overmedication. Nursing home residents are often given psychotropic drugs—50 percent according to some estimates and 80 percent according to others. Geriatricians are concerned that in many cases, no precise diagnosis indicates a need for these powerful drugs and that residents are often overdosed with medications marked "as needed." [According to psychiatrist

Marc E. Agronin], they do not have the benefit of "comprehensive assessment, documentation of diagnosis, and consistent follow-up." Even when a diagnosis of dementia is accurate a very serious problem remains: Psychotropic drugs have not "demonstrated efficacy for most of the behavioral symptoms" shown by nursing home residents who suffer from dementia. In other words, they don't work. Psychotropics are now so common that the American nursing home in the early twenty-first century is more like a psychiatric institution than a medical one. Women who live long enough to be placed in nursing homes may thus be transformed into psychiatric patients, not because of their individual needs or conditions but because they are a captive market for the drug industry. Those with mild dementia may need one or two drugs, but they are almost certain to be given several.

Sedating is a chemical restraint for out-of-control patients, but it is often unnecessary for the majority of nursing home residents. Cultural devaluing of the frail and dependent elderly and the convenience of often underpaid staff may play a larger role in medication decisions than the particular health needs of individual residents.

Gerontologists who write about prescription drugs sometimes use the word "polypharmacy" to refer to multiple drug use. While this term has an authoritatively scientific and neutral sound to it, "polypharmacy" can also be defined as a situation in which a person is given too many drugs, is kept on drugs for too long, or is given "exceedingly high doses." The precise extent of overmedication remains uncertain. The acknowledgment by geriatric pharmacologists that many drugs prescribed for the old are probably unnecessary or ineffective is somewhat misleading because drugs are powerful agents that alter body chemistry; thus they are not "ineffective" in the usual meaning of having no effect.

Nonbiological factors contributing to adverse reactions are drug-swapping by the old, poor doctor-patient communication, and noncompliance on the part of the drug user. Some elderly patients obtain prescriptions from various doctors so that no one doctor or one pharmacist sees the complete picture of their drug consumption. Patients may not tell their doctor what over-the-counter medicines they take. They may not understand, for example, that long-term use of laxatives for constipation can damage their intestines. Others may neglect to mention herbal medications they are on, anticipating the doctor's disapproval. . . . Limited English, hearing loss, extreme deference to doctors, and a sense of powerlessness on the part of the patient are also factors in incomplete drug assessment.

Caution Needed

Doctors who know the most about adverse drug reactions in late life, geriatricians, seem to be the most cautious about prescribing drugs. The majority of old women and men are not treated by these specialists, however. One solution to the problem of overmedication is an increase in the number of geriatricians. Their wise prescribing advice is "start low, go slow."

> *An impartial person might conclude that old people should take* fewer *drugs than others, not more.*

Periodic reevaluation of drugs is crucially important for old people. Drugs should have standard labels giving clear and precise information about how to use them. They now come with inserts that are intended to describe side effects, but inserts typically omit information about the most severe ones. Armed with the full story of their medications' risks, consumers might balk at taking them. It would also be helpful if inserts clearly specified "geriatric dosage." More research is needed to define these doses. Other needed reforms include systematic collection of information about prescribing through computers to eliminate mistakes from illegible handwriting and to allow easier doctor-pharmacist cross-checking of medications.

Juxtaposing the bodily changes with age and adverse drug reactions and taking into account the high cost of medication, an impartial person might conclude that old people should take *fewer* drugs than others, not more. . . .

[According to John le Carré] the drug industry is attempting "the deliberate seduction of the medical profession, country by country, worldwide [and soon] unbought medical opinion will be hard to find." The implications of this judgment for old people who use prescription drugs are ominous.

A closely related problem that has not drawn journalists' attention is that the integrity of gerontology has also been compromised because its conferences and publications are subsidized by pharmaceuticals and therefore papers challenging drug industry hegemony will not be found. Silence about the link between the giant pharmaceuticals and gerontology prevents a critical examination of drugged aging either as a philosophy or as a practice. Journals read by gerontologists and geriatricians feature ads in which dreamy-looking old women (never men) smile out at the reader to show the benefits of tranquilizers. Gerontologists can admit that adverse drug reactions cause thousands of hip fractures each year and other problems causing billions of dollars annually, that one-third of nursing home residents take more than eight drugs a day, and that research on the effects of multiple prescription drug use is lacking, and geriatric nurses can suggest that because of the large number of deaths from adverse drug reactions, noncompliance (failure to take medicines) is sometimes the best choice; but no one can name the present system a public health disaster for old women. . . .

Medical training may reinforce rather than challenge ageist stereotypes. Even when a doctor consciously acknowledges these stereotypes and avoids patronizing behavior, he or she may not be aware of subtle changes in elderly patients caused by medication or may attribute observed changes to the aging process itself rather than to multiple drug use. As a result of all of these factors, establishing the right dosage, guarding against drug interactions, and monitoring use carefully are "beyond the capacity of medicine as it is currently organized." . . .

Social and Cultural Issues

Americans are well known for liking quick fixes, and taking a drug for a medical problem is certainly easier than changing diet, increasing exercise, or reducing stress. This cultural preference for a fast solution may predispose elderly people to expect doctors to prescribe drugs for them and to feel disregarded if they are given none. If they believe they need more drugs than before because they are old, an accumulation of drugs will not prompt questions, especially if their friends who are old also take several a day. A recent commercial for a hotel chain booms "more is better," another American cultural value that encourages over-drugging. . . .

It is logical to suppose that some of what we call "aging" is actually a cumulative reaction to prescription drugs, especially to multiple drugs taken over a long period.

Are the old sedated *because* they are old? [Edith S. Gomberg suggests,] "It may well be that in the minds of legislators and the public, keeping older people sedated is an acceptable idea." How much social control, especially of frail and dependent old people, is appropriate? Do racial and ethnic differences affect drug prescribing and monitoring? Do they affect drug impact? Stanford gerontologist Gwen Yeo cites a study suggesting that old Asian Americans may need only one-half of the drug dose prescribed for whites. Will baby boomers demand more careful drug prescribing as they age?

Is drug coverage through Medicare an adequate solution to high prescription costs for low- and middle-income families? Will old citizens be scapegoated if their consumption of expensive drugs is blamed for driving up health care costs?

Prescription drugs have been in use only since World War II and heavy medication of the old is a fairly recent phenomenon. Thus people now in their eighties have been exposed to drugs for only part of their lives. In twenty years, however, most people will have been in the drug culture all of their lives. Heavy drug use by the old is now so embedded in American culture that a booklet titled *Using Your Medicines Wisely: A Guide for the Elderly*, published by the Department of Health and Human Services, provides space for eleven different drugs to be recorded, in an attractive insert with the remarkably misleading title "Passport to Good Health Care." This official publication sends a subtle but powerful message: Taking eleven different drugs a day is usual and acceptable. This "passport" is a good example of the social construction of aging.

Given the extent and seriousness of adverse drug reactions among people over sixty-five and considering their heavy drug consumption, it is logical to suppose that some of what we call "aging" is actually a cumulative reaction to prescription drugs, especially to multiple drugs taken over a long period. Those who live with elderly relatives and the elderly themselves may well believe that problems they experience result from a slowing-down usual for their age. While some decline is normal for many women and men, drug-induced decline is not, but the two may be hard to separate in America. . . .

Inadequate Science

The most profitable businesses in America promote the myth that aging is a disease for which their product is the appropriate remedy. Pharmaceuticals have joined the tobacco industry as a high-profile threat to the public good. Their practices— the suppression of generic drugs, for example—deserve far more scrutiny.

In a review essay on drugs and the elderly, two medical school professors [Eric Knight and Jerry Avorn] acknowledge that the science underlying current prescription practice is "distressingly thin, especially considering the central roles that medications play in the care of elderly adults and the much-reduced margin for error that makes prescribing for them such a challenge." Pondering this candid assessment might prompt one to ask how drugs became so central to aging, without an adequate science base. The plausible explanation is that culture and the profit motive more than biology or health dictate heavy drug use by people over sixty-five. The primary reason many elders take six or eight drugs a day, or more, is not that their health will benefit but that the drug companies need new markets. An aging population offers more territory for their expanding empires.

The two parts of the statement quoted above, thin science and central roles, collide. What is missing is an admission that the old risk being harmed, perhaps greatly harmed, by current prescribing practice. What is missing is the recognition that drug-induced aging may now pass for normal aging. Older people on medications need to know that the combination of the "thin science" behind the drugs they take and the fat purses of [pharmaceutical companies] Pfizer et al. leaves them open to exploitation and danger. Learning to be old requires keen skepticism about the widespread use of multiple prescription drugs. It may mean questioning one's trust in medical authority for the first time. And families of elders must balance their solicitude for the loved one's well-being with knowledge of the potential dangers of drugs and consider that their parent or grandparent may need far fewer drugs than he or she is on, or no drugs at all.

Many older women and especially women over eighty are needlessly and dangerously overmedicated. In the absence of drug tests designed specifically for old bodies and able to differentiate old women from old men, prescribing multiple drugs for them is a custom that rests more on belief than evidence. The over-drugging of the old is a tragedy of unfathomable proportions. It cries out for a scientist/writer like Rachel Carson [who alerted the public to the dangers of pesticides] to sound the alarm that will wake up Americans of all ages.

Some Nursing Home Elderly Get Futile Care

Associated Press

The Associated Press is an American news agency that produces articles that are used by news outlets throughout the world.

A surprising number of frail, elderly Americans in nursing homes are suffering from futile care at the end of their lives, two new [as of October 2009] federally funded studies reveal.

One found that putting nursing home residents with failing kidneys on dialysis didn't improve their quality of life and may even push them into further decline. The other showed many with advanced dementia will die within six months and perhaps should have hospice care instead of aggressive treatment.

Medical experts say the new research emphasizes the need for doctors, caregivers and families to consider making the feeble elderly who are near death comfortable rather than treating them as if a cure were possible—more like the palliative care given to terminally ill cancer patients.

"We probably need to be offering a palliative care option to many more patients to make the last days of their lives as comfortable as possible," said Dr. Mark Zeidel of the Beth Israel Deaconess Medical Center in Boston, who was not involved in the studies.

Palliative care focuses on managing symptoms of a disease and a main goal is to relieve pain at the end of life.

End-of-life care became a divisive issue in the national health care reform debate this summer [2009] after one proposal included Medicare reimbursement for doctors who consult with patients on end-of-life counseling. Critics called the counseling "death panels" and a step toward euthanasia. The Obama administration denied those claims, yet has signaled the Medicare benefit will be dropped.

New research emphasizes the need for doctors, caregivers and families to consider making the feeble elderly who are near death comfortable rather than treating them as if a cure were possible.

The new studies are published in Thursday's [Oct. 15, 2009's] *New England Journal of Medicine.*

In one study, doctors looked at health records of 3,702 nursing home residents nationwide who started dialysis between 1998 and 2000. The average age was 73 and many had other health problems, including diabetes, heart disease and cancer.

Within the first year, 58 percent died and another 29 percent declined in their ability to do simple tasks such as walking, bathing and getting dressed.

Questionable Benefits

Kidney dialysis helps remove waste from blood, and the vast majority of patients with kidney failure benefit. However, in the case of seniors with failing kidneys, it is less clear whether the benefit outweighs the burden.

The findings call into question the common practice of transporting dialysis patients near the end of life to dialysis centers several times a week and hooking them up to a machine for hours at a time.

"We may be overestimating the benefits of dialysis in some of these patients and downplaying the burdens," said lead author Dr. Manjula Kurella Tamura, a Stanford University kidney specialist.

The study did not include a comparison group of patients who didn't get dialysis, so it's unknown if more elderly are dying after starting dialysis than not. Kurella Tamura said there's no one-size-fits-all recommendation for which nursing home residents should go on dialysis, and she suggests patients talk with their doctors about realistic expectations.

The second study followed 323 people with advanced dementia from Boston-area nursing homes. Their average age was 85 and they could not recognize loved ones and were unable to talk or walk.

One out of four died within six months and half died during the 18 months they were followed. Nursing home residents with advanced dementia were more likely to die of pneumonia, fever and eating problems related to their dementia than from strokes or heart attacks.

During their final three months, 41 percent received aggressive care including being hospitalized and tube feeding. However, if the person making their medical decisions was aware of their poor prognosis, they were less likely to receive aggressive care near the end of life, the research found.

Needless Discomfort

"We often temporarily inflict discomfort or pain on patients. We try to minimize it, but we accept it because we think the trade-off is curing or healing," said Dr. Greg Sachs of Indiana University School of Medicine.

In an accompanying editorial, Sachs recalled how his grandmother, who suffered from Alzheimer's [disease] and lived in a nursing home, was aggressively treated with antibiotics for every infection in her final months and had to be restrained. He said that people with dementia could benefit from hospice care inside a nursing home or in the community.

Sachs cited research that found nursing home residents who had hospice care during the last month of their lives were half as likely to be hospitalized. What's keeping dementia nursing home patients from getting hospice care is that dementia is not widely recognized as a terminal illness. It's also harder to predict when a dementia patient has six months or less to live—a criteria for Medicare-paid hospice care.

The National Institutes of Health funded the studies. The dementia study was led by the Harvard-affiliated Hebrew SeniorLife Institute for Aging Research in Boston. In the dialysis study, Kurella Tamura has received grant support from Amgen, which makes a drug for people with kidney disease undergoing dialysis.

High-Tech Care for People over Eighty Is Too Costly to Be Justified

Daniel Callahan

Daniel Callahan is a senior research scholar and president emeritus of the Hastings Center, a nonprofit bioethics research institute. He is the author or editor of more than forty books.

The most important aim of a health care system should be to help a person go from being a young person to becoming an old person. However, once a person has achieved that goal, there ought to be a reduced obligation on the part of a health care system to help someone become indefinitely older, much less as old as that person might like. A full life, I believe, can be achieved by most people sometime between the ages of 70 and 80, and the health care system should aim to make the years between birth and that age range its main goal. After age 80, which is the outer (but not inflexible) limit for policy purpose, the priority should shift from the cure of disease and acute care medicine to the provision of good long-term and home care, together with solid rehabilitation and income support. As it presently happens, acute care costs for the elderly decline after age 80, but it is reasonable to expect that these costs will rise with a (likely) more demanding patient baby boom population.

In an earlier book, I spoke of a "natural life span," suggesting the late 70s or early 80s as the time when most people would have achieved such a span. Well, the word "natural" brings out hives in some people, and it was commonly noted that, with increasingly extended life expectancies, there is no biologically fixed length of life and thus no "natural" life span.

The notion of a "full life" better captures what I was trying to say. It is a phrase that I have frequently heard used to describe the breadth of experience that an elderly person has had by the end of life. I take it to mean that someone has had the chance to live a life long enough to enjoy most, although not necessarily all, of the pleasures and satisfactions that we can get from living a life: love, education, parenthood, travel, a work life, friendship, and many social activities.

After age 80 . . . the priority should shift from the cure of disease and acute care medicine to the provision of good long-term and home care.

To object that we are all different and have a wide range of values, aims, and hopes about our lives is true. But we are all not *so* different that no generalizations are possible, valid for most people if not for all. Some people, it is true, would like to run marathons at age 90 and do so. But most of us have no such aims, and, in any event, it is hardly self-evident that it is the duty of a health care system to make such ambitions possible or, indeed, that the elderly marathon aspirant at age 90 would have had less than a full life for failing to run because of bad knees. I would like to travel to Nepal, but the absence of such a trip would hardly make my life a failure and less than full because of that omission. Our individual definitions of a full life should not be the norm for national health policy. That is the economically corrosive core of our present system, for Medicare, as well as for the entire system. The health norm should aim, as do all responsible public policies, to find a reasonable way to help us all in a collective manner that takes account of our most common needs and aspirations when it cannot meet all of them. Public policy cannot deliver boutique health care.

In earlier societies, with shorter life expectancies, a "full life" could have been achieved in a shorter period of time, and thus, the length of life and its fullness were not necessarily identical. Do we look back on the deaths of the founding fathers of our country, mainly in their 60s and 70s, as a national tragedy, as if they had died prematurely, their lives incomplete, their lives less than full? No one has ever, so far as I know, said that, and why should they? One can, however, say that it was a tragedy that so many women of that eighteenth century era died in childbirth and that so many of the children of that era did not survive to adulthood.

Drawing on Experience

I present the notion of a "full life" as a social and experiential concept, based on my own observation and experience of living a long life and of trying to make sense of the different stages of life and the varied reactions to them. In any case, it is open to my readers to compare my observations with those of their own. My suggestion of 80 years as an upper boundary is of course in one sense arbitrary—why not 79 or 81? But for policy purposes, it represents a reasonable number, much the same as the age of 65 was a reasonable number for Medicare eligibility, or 16 for a driver's license, or 21 for drinking alcoholic beverages. I do not mean for that particular age to be used as a rigid standard, much less written into law. I see it instead as a strong signal to patients, families, and physicians to shift gears, raising the bar for aggressive technological interventions, which a use of QALYs [quality-adjusted life years, a measure used in estimating the cost effectiveness of a medical treatment] will bring about, but also in ways that take account of patient and disease differences.

I first began thinking about the idea of a full life at funerals, noting the great difference in the reaction of those gathered to honor the deceased depending on his or her age at death. I have rarely noticed signs of strong grief and weeping at the funeral of those over 80, and often not even at funerals of those over 70. My mother died at age 86, and those who came to her funeral did not cry but, instead, spoke about how much they liked her, what a fine person she had been, how she had lived a "full" life, and said that she "would be missed." The funerals of young children or adult parents with small children are entirely different (one of our own children died). Grief overcomes most of those who come (and they come in much greater numbers), and it is hard not to cry.

Some people, it is true, would like to run marathons at age 90 and do so. But ... it is hardly self-evident that it is the duty of a health care system to make such ambitions possible.

Why is there that difference? I think that it is no accident, and that we know through our experience and observation the difference between someone who had not lived a long and full life, who still had many significant stages of life and experience before them and one who has not. The latter is what we mean by a "premature death." There is, moreover, a difference between a death that is tragic and one that is sad but expected and accepted, and that is the fundamental difference between the death of the young and the old. Another influence on my thinking has been the reading of obituaries for many years, a habit that grows with age, and particularly when one's own age group begins to gradually die off. It is hard to think that someone who has lived into his or her eighth decade, who once pursued and then retired from a career, who had children and grandchildren, had not lived a full life even if there were a few more things that person might have wished to do.

I call my idea of a "full life" a quasi-empirical concept; that is, it is based on my observations, its frequent use by others in our society, and because it helps to explain some phenomenon of aging and death that does not seem otherwise explicable. For thinking this way, I have been called a "mortalist" and an "apologist," someone who seems to fatalistically accept aging and death instead of taking full arms against them. I plead guilty to the charge. I cannot imagine running a long-term affordable and sustainable health care system without a citizenry that is willing to accept aging and death, even though with ambivalence and reluctance.

Aging Is Not a Disease

The push by "transhumanists," for a much-extended human life expectancy of 150 years and more is no help to our common future and surely a seductive distraction from decent care for the elderly. The idea that death is just a correctible biological accident and aging a conquerable disease like any other, are the ideas of a small, but growing, minority. But I suspect they have some influence beyond their numbers, attractive to a culture looking for medical miracles and fed a steady diet of hope and hype. A British sociologist [John A. Vincent] has made a good case that utopians who want to carry a "war" against old age "share a dominant cultural view that devalues old age and old people."

I cannot imagine running a long-term affordable and sustainable health care system without a citizenry that is willing to accept aging and death.

When I was earlier criticized for wanting to use age as a decision-making standard, I often responded with two questions, which hardly anyone took the trouble to answer. If you do not like age to count in determining treatment, does that mean that the elderly are to be entitled to any and all treatments regardless of the cost and that the 9-year-old must compete for lifesaving resources against the 90-year-old on a level economic playing field? Or does it mean that an expensive treatment at age 85 that ensures only a few extra months of life should be provided? No one seemed quite prepared to say that; but neither did anyone offer an alternative standard. Questions of that kind make everyone uncomfortable. They put the cost problem to the ultimate test, which is one reason why trying to mix the cost of health care and our commitment to the value of life is acutely discomforting.

I have frequently asked my critics this question: If you think my approach is harsh—even though you agree there is a problem that will get all the worse as the baby boomers retire—tell me what your harsh solution is? No one has ever offered such a solution. They have proffered instead sweet, Alice-in-Wonderland alternatives: more and better medical research to cure the diseases of the elderly, programs to cut waste and inefficiency, dreamy scenarios of modernized lifestyles for the elderly, and do not believe future cost projections anyway. At least at age 79, no one is likely to ask me, as all did 20 years ago, whether I would still think that way when I was old. Getting rid of questions like that is one of the benefits of old age. To be sure, it could be said that, at 79, I am like most elderly people set in at least a few old-fashioned ways, unable to entertain new possibilities, fresh and transformed ways of thinking about, and living, old age. That may well be true, but it does not alter the fact that my feelings on the subject have only become intensified with age, living with it myself.

Excessive Treatment of People Dying of Old Age Is Cruel

Craig Bowron

Craig Bowron is a hospital-based internist and a writer in St. Paul, Minnesota.

It's January [2009], and with the holidays behind us, here in Minnesota the deep psychosis of winter settles in. The cold has a sharper edge; the darkness of night seems more penetrating and brittle. We'll take the ornaments off the tree but leave the lights on and keep watering it until it gives up its photosynthetic ghost. The green must be cherished until life returns in earnest in the spring.

I'm a physician in a large hospital in Minneapolis, where I help care for patients struggling through the winter of their lives. We've got a lively spring unit, an obstetrical ward where fresh-faced tulips are popping up at all hours, but that's not my specialty. As a hospitalist, I see adult patients of all ages and complexities, most of whom make good recoveries and return to life as they knew it. But taking care of the thread worn elderly, those facing an eternal winter with no green in sight, is definitely the most difficult thing I do.

That's because never before in history has it been so hard to fulfill our final earthly task: dying. It used to be that people were "visited" by death. With nothing to fight it, we simply accepted it and grieved. Today, thanks to myriad medications and interventions that have been created to improve our health and prolong our lives, dying has become a difficult and often excruciatingly slow process.

Suffering Patients

Take one of my patients. She started dialysis six months ago at the tender age of 85, and the diabetic vascular problems that put her kidneys in the tank persist. One leg has been amputated above the knee, and several toes on her remaining foot have succumbed to gangrene. Robbed of blood, they appear dry, black and tenuously connected, like an ash dangling off a cigarette.

Today, thanks to myriad medications and interventions . . . dying has become a difficult and often excruciatingly slow process.

This patient was brought in for a decreased level of consciousness and low blood pressure, but she has been having periods of nausea, and her appetite seems to have died with her kidneys. The initial workup revealed little, perhaps a low-grade bladder infection, but treating it and her low blood pressure doesn't seem to make much of a difference. She is withdrawn; food goes into her mouth, but she won't chew and swallow unless her children instruct her to. She intermittently refuses pills. There's a language barrier, but her children are there to interpret for her. Translation: She feels exhausted and weak, and she feels that way most of the time.

This woman is suffering from what we call "the dwindles," characterized by advancing age and illness. Although dialysis is a miraculous technology—she'd be dead without it—it exacts a heavy toll from someone her age or with her medical problems. Three days a week are spent in dialysis, and the other four are spent recovering. It is extending her life, but she's miserable.

Her family has designated her "full code," meaning that if her heart stopped or she were to cease breathing, we would do CPR to revive her, even though there would be a very slim chance of success—and even though it would be God's or the universe's way of giving her an easy way out.

Another patient is in even worse shape. He's 91 and still a very big man. When I enter his room to examine him, he seems like a giant oak felled into a hospital bed, stiff and rigid, with swollen arthritic joints. A stroke four months earlier paralyzed his right side and left him bed-bound and nearly helpless, with pressure sores on his heels. He is mildly demented, and the pain pills aren't helping. He was brought to the ER [emergency room] because he was thought to be having another stroke, though these new symptoms quickly resolved.

Talking with this patient, I recognize his race and the Cajun accent; I'm certain that I took care of him sometime in the past, but he is not the man he was then. Staring at his 230 pounds stretching the length of the bed, I wonder how difficult it must be to care for him. To transfer him to a toilet or a chair requires the use of a Hoyer lift, a gigantic sling that's wrapped around the patient and attached to a mobile mini-crane. Fully suspended, he looks like a massive baby being delivered by a giant stork. The contortions and gymnastics of getting him slung up and moved must drive him wild with arthritic pain.

Though I reviewed the patient's chart before going into his room, I can't recall seeing what nursing facility he had come from. So, I ask the nurse. She tells me, unbelievably, that he has come from his home, where his son cares for him. Later in the day I place a call to this Clark Kent, this Superman in disguise.

The son answers with soft echoes of his father's Louisiana brogue, and I ask him how in the world he manages to take care of his dad. He replies that for one, it's all he does, a full-time job, and moreover, his experiences in Vietnam numbed him to some of the intimacies of caring for another human being. "Once you've shoved some guy's guts back into his stomach, you know, you can get used to the rest of it," he says.

Hard to Watch

He tells me that his father is wearing out and that it's hard to watch. The arthritis has become quite painful, and sometimes his dad just weeps. Some nights he needs a couple of Vicodin to be able to sleep through the pain. The old man is also spending a lot more time thinking about his wife, who passed away before him. His son thinks he may be ready to die.

Nothing in my medical training qualifies me to judge what kind of life is satisfying or worth living. Many would say that if we were to become paralyzed in an accident, just let us die. But many quadriplegics, once they've gone through an initial period of adjustment, find their lives very satisfying. Patients can and do make enormous efforts and fight precipitous odds to get back to life as they knew it, or even just to go on living. But the difference for many elderly is that what's waiting for them at the end of this illness is just another illness, and another struggle.

Another patient of mine has 86 years behind her and was brought to our hospital from a nursing home in the wee hours of the morning. Her diabetes has become very brittle and difficult to control; the day before, paramedics were called because her blood sugar had dipped so low that she was becoming unresponsive. She also has dementia, and a couple of months ago, she fell and broke a hip. Although it was repaired and she completed rehabilitation, she has wound up essentially bedridden. Strictly speaking, losing your mind won't kill you: It's the falling, the choking, the weakness, the bedsores.

This patient was brought in because the nursing home staff thought that she might have aspirated some food or secretions and developed pneumonia. She thinks it's 1982 and is, as we say, "pleasantly confused." She denies any and all symptoms, and her breathing looks comfortable. A review of her chart shows no fever and a normal white blood cell count. Her chest X-ray shows perhaps a subtle pneumonia but also a compression fracture of one of her vertebrae, which has gone from being 50 percent to 90 percent collapsed. Her dementia has mercifully spared her a lot of pain from the fracture, but it also keeps her from recognizing members of her extended family. Sometimes she doesn't recognize her own son, who drove to the hospital to be with her at this early hour.

He and I discuss what brought her in, and then we talk about her code status, which he confirms is Do Not Resuscitate. "She wasn't supposed to be brought to the hospital in the first place," the son tells me, and puzzled, I ask him to say that again. She was never supposed to be hospitalized: Whatever troubles arrived, the plan was to deal with them in the nursing home. His mother had made that decision herself, several years prior to this hospitalization, before the dementia really set in.

Later that day, I meet with the son and a few other close family members. They want to continue the medications that would bring their mother comfort and discontinue all the rest. They aren't looking to end her life, but they aren't looking to prolong it, either. They can see that she is moving away from them in both body and mind, and they are ready to let her go.

For many elderly ... what's waiting for them at the end of this illness is just another illness, and another struggle.

Prolonging the Torture

To be clear: Everyone dies. There are no lifesaving medications, only life-prolonging ones. To say that anyone chooses to die is, in most situations, a misstatement of the facts. But medical advances have created at least the facade of choice. It appears as if death has made a counteroffer and that the responsibility is now ours.

In today's world, an elderly person or their family must "choose," for example, between dialysis and death, or a feeding tube and death. Those can be very simple choices when you're

40 and critically ill; they can be agonizing when you're 80 and the bad days outnumber the good days two to one.

It's not hard to identify one of these difficult cases in the hospital. Among the patient-care team—nurses, physicians, nursing assistants, physical and occupational therapists, etc.— there is often a palpable sense of "What in the world are we doing to this patient?" That's "to" and not "for." We all stagger under the weight of feeling complicit in a patient's torture, but often it's the nurses who bear most of that burden, physically and emotionally. As a nurse on a dialysis floor told me, "They'll tell us things that they won't tell the family or their physician. They'll say, 'I don't want to have any more dialysis. I'm tired of it,' but they won't admit that to anyone else."

This sense of complicity is what makes taking care of these kinds of patients the toughest thing I do. A fellow physician told me, "I feel like I am participating in something immoral." Another asked, "Whatever happened to that 'do no harm' business?"

There is often a palpable sense of "What in the world are we doing to this patient?"

If we can be honest and admit that we have no choice about dying, then the only things we do have a say in are the circumstances. Like many nursing home patients, Dorothy was on the cholesterol-lowering medication Lipitor. Why? So that she wouldn't die of a heart attack or a stroke. But don't we all die of something?

Everyone wants to grow old and die in his or her sleep, but the truth is that most of us will die in pieces. Most will be nibbled to death by piranhas, and the piranhas of senescence are wearing some very dull dentures. It can be a torturously slow process, with an undeniable end, and our instinct shouldn't be to prolong it. If you were to walk by a Tilt-A-Whirl [an amusement park ride] loaded with elderly riders and notice that all of them were dizzy to the point of vomiting, wouldn't your instinct be to turn the ride off? Or at the very least slow it down? Mercy calls for it.

This isn't about euthanasia. It's not about spiraling health care costs. It's about the gift of life—and death. It is about living life and death with dignity, and letting go.

In the past, the facade of immortality was claimed by Egyptian kings, egomaniacal monarchs and run-of-the-mill psychopaths. But democracy and modern medical advances have made the illusion accessible to everyone. We have to rid ourselves of this distinctly Western notion before our nation's obesity epidemic and the surge of aging baby boomers combine to form a tsunami of infirmity that may well topple our hospital system and wash it out to sea.

At some point in life, the only thing worse than dying is being kept alive.

CHAPTER 4

What Major Problems Are Common Among the Elderly?

Chapter Preface

Although the majority of elderly Americans live comfortably, some face serious problems. People who are aware of these problems sometimes overestimate their extent and assume that they are typical, thus gaining an unrealistically depressing view of old age. On the other hand, the public often shuts out awareness of the very real suffering of all too many people past a certain age, expecting that it will pass.

Nearly one in six adults over the age of sixty-five has an income either below or close to the official U.S. poverty line. More than 2.5 million are at risk of hunger, and many actually experience it. To be sure, this means that more than 83 percent of people over sixty-five are *not* poor; it cannot be said that the elderly, as a group, tend to live in poverty. Some, in fact, have ample savings and are affluent. However, the tragic situation of the minority—many of whom worked hard for their entire lives—cannot be ignored.

The poor and the hungry can be found among adults of all ages, but for the elderly, the situation seems worse because they cannot anticipate a better future. Younger people who are poor can hope that they will get a good job someday and will eventually rise out of poverty. Many of the elderly poor are physically unable to work, and those capable of working often find it impossible to get jobs. If they do get jobs, they are usually low-paying, uninteresting occupations that do not utilize their skills and past experience. Teens don't mind working in fast-food restaurants because they don't expect to do it for the rest of their lives. Elderly people who must work there know that they will probably continue until their active lives come to an end.

The saddest and most horrifying situations of the elderly arise after their active lives are indeed over, and they are physically and/or mentally disabled. Elder abuse is a growing problem—one that until recently was largely hidden but now is receiving more attention. Although physical abuse in nursing homes attracts the most publicity, it is far from the most common form. Only a small percentage of the elderly live in nursing homes; most elder abuse—physical, emotional, financial, and even sexual—occurs in aged people's own homes. It is not confined to those with low income; stressed-out family members as well as well-paid caregivers and con artists take advantage of wealthy elders, too. Vulnerable when disabled, they have no way to escape and are often afraid to report betrayal by those on whom they depend. Again, this is not something experienced by the majority, many of whom are cared for by loving families. That elder abuse occurs at all, however, is appalling.

The one insurmountable problem that does confront most elderly people sooner or later is the prolonged process of dying. In the past, final illnesses were typically short. Now, because of advances in medicine that delay death, a long period of increasing helplessness—often requiring nursing home care, which means misery for the patient and impoverishment for the family—can occur. Nearly 50 percent of people over the age of eighty-five—the fastest-growing segment of the elderly population—eventually develop Alzheimer's disease or some other form of dementia, and as more diseases become preventable or curable, this proportion will grow.

Whether or not a person has been in a nursing home, his or her life generally ends in a hospital, although most Americans say they would rather die at home. The elderly rarely die suddenly in their sleep, and when life-threatening symptoms strike, no alternative to hospitalization exists unless full-time skilled caregivers are available. People can specify in advance what measures they do or do not want taken in the hospital to postpone an inevitable death, but this is seldom done, and in the absence of such instructions, the elderly sometimes are subjected to pointless, and even painful, treatment.

People of all ages close their eyes to these facts, although a movement toward publicizing them is growing. Despite current attempts to deal with the problems, they cannot be entirely eliminated. Though much can—and should—be done to help elderly individuals who suffer from poverty, abuse, or end-of-life issues, the realities of aging are inherent in the course of living. Nearly everyone will someday be elderly, which is a thought many would like to avoid. Still, few would seriously wish never to be old, considering that the only alternative is to die young.

Poverty Among the Elderly Is Widespread in America

Ellen O'Brien, Ke Bin Wu, and David Baer

Ellen O'Brien is a senior strategic policy advisor at the Public Policy Institute of AARP, an advocacy organization for older Americans. Ke Bin Wu and David Baer are policy research analysts at the Public Policy Institute.

Poverty among the elderly remains a serious and persistent problem in the United States. Nearly one in ten adults age 65 and above live in a family with income below the official U.S. poverty line, or federal poverty level (FPL). In 2008, an adult age 65 and older living alone was counted as poor if his or her annual cash income before taxes was below $10,326. An elderly couple with income below $13,014 was counted as poor. Nearly one in six older adults was poor or near poor, with income below 125 percent of the FPL and about a third had low income—below 200 percent of the FPL.

The fact that 3.7 million older adults do not have sufficient cash income to meet their basic expenses too often escapes attention. By most accounts, elderly poverty is a problem we have largely solved. Since 1968 the poverty rate among adults age 65 and older has declined by about a third, falling from 25 percent in 1968 to 9.7 percent in 2008. In contrast, poverty among younger adults, and especially among children, has risen in recent decades even as national prosperity, real gross domestic product per capita, has grown. But poverty—particularly poverty among the elderly—is mismeasured and poverty rates are still unacceptably high, especially for certain groups of older Americans.

Some Groups Are Hit Harder than Others

Poverty hits some groups of older adults more than others. Twenty percent of older adults who are black or Hispanic are poor, and poverty hits people with limited education and those who are not married especially hard. Most poor adults age 65 and older are not married—either widowed (43 percent), divorced or separated (19 percent), or never married (8 percent). Older women of color are especially likely to live in poverty. Nearly a quarter of older women who are black or Hispanic are poor, and more than a third are poor or near poor (with income below 125 percent of the FPL).

The fact that 3.7 million older adults do not have sufficient cash income to meet their basic expenses too often escapes attention.

Poverty among older adults varies across the states, but because of Social Security and Supplemental Security Income (SSI)—which provide uniform federal benefits—the percentage of older adults living in poverty varies far less across the country than the percentage of children living in poverty. The percentage of older adults living in poverty in 2008 ranged from a high of 16.9 percent in Mississippi to a low of 3.7 percent in Alaska.

Most poor older adults receive income from Social Security. In fact, the majority (59 percent) of poor older adults depend on Social Security for all or nearly all (90 percent or more) of their family income. And although Social Security benefits are typically large enough to prevent older people from living in poverty, some people receive only modest benefits that leave them in poverty. Older poor families are substantially less likely than the nonpoor to have income from assets, earnings, and pensions. And, even when they do have income from these sources, poor families derive less from these sources of income than do nonpoor families. Only about

15 percent of poor older families received cash assistance from SSI or other cash welfare programs.

An array of state and federal assistance programs is available to assist poor and low-income older adults, but a substantial share of even very low-income adults do not benefit from programs that could supplement limited incomes and make food, shelter, utilities, health care, and other necessities more affordable. Many of the elderly poor receive assistance from other (noncash or near-cash) federal assistance programs, including Medicaid and the Medicare Savings Programs (MSPs), the Medicare Part D low-income subsidy (LIS), and the Supplemental Nutrition Assistance Program (SNAP, formerly food stamps).

Many older adults who live in poor families face other challenges that make it especially difficult to get by on a limited income. Poor older adults tend to be in worse health than adults who are not poor: They tend to have more chronic and disabling health conditions. Poor health and disability, on top of very limited income and inadequate insurance protection, mean that health care costs are a burden for many poor older adults. In 2009, the typical poor adult age 65 and older spent 19.6 percent of income on health care, compared to 6.1 percent for older adults with incomes above 400 percent of poverty. Health care costs are unaffordable (exceed 20 percent of family income) for half of poor elderly adults.

Housing Costs Are Unaffordable

Housing takes an even bigger bite out of the incomes of poor older adults. The median poor older household spent 60 percent of annual household income on housing in 2007. Put another way, housing costs are extremely unaffordable (absorbing more than half of household income) for more than half (56.9 percent) of older poor households. When a less restrictive standard is used, more than three-fourths of poor older households faced a housing affordability problem, spending more than 30 percent of household income on housing in 2008.

Food is a far less costly item than housing in the budgets of the elderly poor, but a growing share of poor and near-poor older households experienced severe difficulties paying for food in 2008. In 2008, 22.1 percent of low-income elderly households (with incomes below 130 percent of the poverty line) were "food insecure" (they had limited or uncertain availability of nutritionally adequate and safe foods or limited or uncertain ability to acquire acceptable foods). This is a substantial increase from 2006, when 17.6 percent of the very low-income elderly had low or very low food security.

Some of the elderly poor can draw on assets to ease their hardships. Some poor older adults may have accumulated assets that can provide a cushion during hard times and can be used to meet extraordinary needs. But most have few assets, and most of what they do have is tied up in their home. Poor older adults had median assets (excluding home equity) of just $5,310 in 2005. Even when home equity is included, the median total family assets of elderly poor individuals were just $66,600 in 2005.

Poor older adults tend to be in worse health than adults who are not poor.

The official U.S. poverty measure has been in use for more than four decades, but increasingly, it fails to accurately describe who is and who is not poor, and it does an especially inadequate job of measuring the extent of poverty among older adults. Nearly twice as many adults age 65 and above are poor when newer measurement approaches are used.

Reducing poverty among older adults should be a policy priority for federal and state policy makers. Options for alleviating poverty among the elderly include improvements in Social Security and SSI, better protection from high out-of-pocket costs for health care and long-term care, and policies to ensure that housing is affordable for both renters and homeowners.

Homelessness Is Increasing Among Elderly Adults

M William Sermons and Meghan Henry

M William Sermons is the director of the Homelessness Research Institute of the National Alliance to End Homelessness. Meghan Henry was a research associate at the institute.

There is some troubling evidence that homelessness is beginning to increase among elderly adults. In addition, there are demographic factors—such as the anticipated growth of the elderly population as baby boomers turn 65 years of age and recent reports of increases in the number of homeless adults ages 50 to 64—that suggest a dramatic increase in the elderly homeless population between 2010 and 2020. While the country's changing demographics may make this finding unsurprising, it has serious implications for providers of homeless services and should be deeply troubling to the policy makers that aim to prevent poverty and homelessness among the elderly through local and federal social welfare programs. . . .

Homelessness Among the Elderly

While there is a fair amount known about elders experiencing poverty and about the general homeless population, there is relatively little known about the elderly homeless population. This section details what we know from existing research about incidence and growth of homelessness among the elderly.

The elderly population has historically been underrepresented among the homeless population. The limited national homelessness data that have been collected over the past two decades are consistent in revealing that homelessness is much more prevalent among younger adults than among older adults and the elderly. A 1996 national study by the Urban Institute found that, while those over age 55 represented 28 percent of the general adult population, they made up only 8 percent of the homeless population. This underrepresentation is also reflected in HUD's [Department of Housing and Urban Development's] 2008 annual homelessness data, which reveal that the incidence of sheltered homelessness among adults over 18 years of age is 55 per 10,000, while the annual incidence among those ages 62 and older is 9 per 10,000. While these findings speak to the relative infrequency of homelessness among the elderly, any level of homelessness among the elderly is concerning.

Homelessness among elderly persons will increase substantially over the next decade.

There is very limited national data on the changing demographics of the homeless population, but the data that do exist show that homelessness among the elderly and older adults is modestly increasing. . . .

Homelessness among elderly persons will increase substantially over the next decade. There are two primary demographic factors that contribute to the projected increase in homelessness among the elderly. One is the overall growth in the elderly population, which is expected to more than double in size between now [April 2010] and 2050. The other factor is the relative stability in the proportion of the elderly population facing economic vulnerability. Together, these factors signal an increase in elder economic vulnerability and homelessness.

The Growing Elderly Population

There are more Americans over the age of 65 today than ever before and the number is rapidly increasing. During the past century, the number of elderly people has grown from 3.1 million in 1900 to 37 million in 2008—an increase of over 1,100 percent. The population of elderly Americans has also increased since 1900, when adults ages 65 and older made up only 4.1 percent of the population. Today, at 37 million, elderly Americans make up 12.6 percent of the population. This demographic shift means that we have become an older nation, with the median age at almost 37 years old—the country's highest median age on record. Further, the U.S. Census Bureau projects that by 2050 there will be approximately 89 million people over the age of 65, which more than doubles our current elderly population. This projected increase in elderly Americans merits significant attention at the federal policy level. An increased number of elderly persons will mean an increased need for federal programs aimed at preventing economic vulnerability among older persons.

Economic Vulnerability Among the Elderly

The most common measure of economic instability among the elderly is poverty.... According to the 2008 American Community Survey, 9.9 percent of people over 65 years of age had annual incomes below the poverty threshold of $10,326 for a single person and $13,030 for a couple.

A measure of even greater economic vulnerability is the proportion of elderly persons in deep poverty—earning only half of the poverty threshold. In 2008, there were over 969,925 elderly persons, or 2.6 percent of the elderly population, in deep poverty.... Federal programs such as Social Security, Supplemental Nutrition Assistance Programs (formerly known as the Food Stamp Program), and housing programs directed to the elderly have helped decrease the number of persons over 65 years of age living in precarious housing situations due to insufficient income. Despite the overall effectiveness of these programs, some elderly people are not prevented from experiencing economic hardship and homelessness. . . .

Because of anticipated increases in the elderly homeless population as the general population ages, a projection of the elderly homeless population [has been made] based on the following assumptions:

- The elderly population will increase as projected by the U.S. Census Bureau through 2050.

- The rate of deep poverty in the elderly population will remain constant at 2 percent through 2050, as it has remained since 1975.

- The 2008 ratio of 1 sheltered elderly homeless person to every 22 elderly persons in deep poverty remains constant through 2050.

With rising housing costs, elderly households often must choose between housing and other basic needs such as food and medical care.

Homelessness is projected to increase by 33 percent from 44,172 in 2010 to 58,772 in 2020 and will more than double between 2010 and 2050, when over 95,000 elderly persons are projected to be homeless.

This projected increase in homelessness among elderly persons is alarming. . . .

Precariously Housed Elderly Households

At its root, homelessness is the result of an inability to afford housing. With rising housing costs, elderly households often must choose between housing and other basic needs such as food and medical care. Housing cost burden exists when a household pays more than 30 percent of [its] income on housing costs. This burden is considered "severe" when the portion of a household's income dedicated to housing exceeds 50 percent. This housing expense can leave a household economically vulnerable. This is particularly concerning for elderly people who often rely on a fixed income. In 2007, over 8.7 million households with a householder over the age of 65 experienced housing cost burden. This represents 38 percent of all households with an elderly householder. Further, over 4.8 million of them experienced severe housing cost burden, accounting for approximately 21 percent of total elderly households.

Meeting the needs of [the elderly] population, particularly the economically vulnerable portion of the population, will be one of the greatest domestic policy challenges in our lifetime.

In recent years, the increase in the rate of severe cost burden among elderly households has outpaced the overall growth of elderly households. While the share of total households headed by a person over the age of 65 remained relatively unchanged between 2001 and 2007, the percent of elderly households experiencing a severe housing cost burden increased by over 14 percent. Further, while elderly households constituted over one-quarter (26 percent) of the total number of severely cost-burdened households in 2007, they accounted for only 20 percent of total households. This overrepresentation of severely cost-burdened elderly households among all households, as well as the faster rate of growth among severely cost-burdened elderly households, has significant policy implications. Federal housing policy should be expanded and adjusted to meet the needs of poor and vulnerable Americans—who increasingly are our elderly. . . .

Elderly chronically homeless people often require intensive service coordination. This helps them transition into permanent housing smoothly and ensures they remain there. Case management is often critical in coordinating care—primary health care, housing assistance, food, and other services can get lost without some assistance and supervision. Elderly homeless people often face barriers to accessing resources and benefits such as Social Security, Medicare, and Supplemental Security Income (SSI). They may not know that they are eligible for such benefits, they may not know where to start, and/or they may have a hard time following up with service providers, meeting appointments, or completing the necessary paperwork due to health limitations (mental or physical). A coordination of services, coupled with housing assistance, can help homeless or formerly homeless seniors age in their own housing with dignity. . . .

A Call to Action and Inquiry

In the coming years, the United States will experience a monumental societal shift as baby boomers become senior citizens. Meeting the needs of this population, particularly the economically vulnerable portion of the population, will be one of the greatest domestic policy challenges in our lifetime. Social Security, Medicare, and housing programs targeting the elderly will be critical for meeting the challenge and reducing risk of homelessness. Below is a list of recommendations to reduce and eventually eliminate homelessness among elderly persons in the United States.

1. *Increase the supply of subsidized affordable housing on which economically vulnerable elderly persons rely.* In addition to the Section 202 Supportive Housing for the Elderly Program, elderly persons also make up either the majority or a large fraction of the beneficiaries of the other federal affordable rental housing programs— public housing, Housing Choice Voucher Program (Section 8), Project-Based Section 8, and the Section 515

Rural Rental Housing Program. These programs must be preserved and expanded to keep pace with expected increases in demand and to provide a way of providing housing stability for the tens of thousands of elderly persons who experience homelessness every year. Capitalization of the National Housing Trust Fund, which will be used to build, rehabilitate and preserve housing for the lowest-income households, will be a critical element of ensuring that the programs upon which elderly persons depend are adequately sized.

2. *Create sufficient permanent supportive housing to finish the job of ending chronic homelessness.* The aging of the chronically homeless population from the older adult to the elderly age group is one of the ways that homelessness among elderly persons is expected to grow in the coming years. This pathway can be largely averted if the job of ending chronic homelessness is successfully completed in the next 10 years. This requires the creation of sufficient supportive housing units to house the approximately 120,000 persons who are chronically homeless today. Because of the progressive health care and support needs of this population, it is critical that this population receives housing combined with flexible and adaptive support services.

3. *Research to better understand the needs of the homeless elderly population.* One of the recurrent themes of this paper is the paucity of information available about the elderly homeless population. Research is needed to better understand the characteristics of the population. Specifically, research is needed into the patterns of homeless and mainstream service utilization, the frequency and duration of homeless episodes, and health status and functionality of elderly homeless people. This information is necessary to form a typology of the elderly homeless population that can be used to better plan

and target effective interventions, including supportive housing and homelessness prevention strategies.

The existence of homelessness among the elderly indicates that our safety nets are failing our most vulnerable citizens. However, with thoughtful and strategic planning, we can greatly reduce elderly homelessness and prevent the population at risk from experiencing homelessness. Addressing the unmet housing and service needs of our at-risk and homeless elderly, as well as understanding the characteristics and needs of the elderly population at risk of homelessness can help us end elder homelessness. As a nation, we are judged by how we care for our most vulnerable citizens. It is a failing of public policy that any of our elderly are homeless. To fail to act would be, in short, irresponsible.

Some People Must Continue to Work in Old Age, Yet Cannot Find Jobs

Clare Ansberry

Clare Ansberry is the Pittsburgh bureau chief for the Wall Street Journal *and a winner of the Darrell Sifford Memorial Prize in Journalism.*

Mary Appleby, 76 years old, lost her job in January [2009] as a cashier at a courthouse cafeteria here [Akron, OH]. She is now looking for minimum-wage work.

Mary Bennett, 80, began filling out applications for fast-food restaurants and convenience stores after she was laid off last March as a machinist. Fred Dase, 81, a bartender until last summer, also needs another job.

During past recessions, older workers simply would have retired rather than searching want ads and applying for jobs. But these days, with outstanding mortgages, bank loans and high medical bills, many of them can't afford to be out of work.

With jobs so scarce, people in their seventh and eighth decades are up against those half their age in a desperate scramble for work.

The number of unemployed workers 75 and older increased to more than 73,000 in January, up 46% from the prior January. Among workers 65 and older, the jobless rate stands at 5.7%. That's below the national average, but well above what it was in previous recessions, including the recession of 1981, when it reached 4.3%.

The growing numbers reflect, in part, an increase in the number of older workers. The percentage of people 65 and older who are in the workforce rose to 16.8% at year-end, from 11.9% a decade earlier. Among people 75 and older, the increase was even greater—to 7.3%, from 4.7%.

These days, with outstanding mortgages, bank loans and high medical bills, many [elderly people] can't afford to be out of work.

Financial Necessity

As people live longer and stay in better health, some of them merely want the stimulation and challenge of a job. But for workers like Ms. Appleby, Ms. Bennett and Mr. Dase, the motivation is financial necessity.

Fewer people than in years past are covered by defined-benefit plans, such as company-sponsored pensions that guarantee them specific monthly income for life. Those with retirement investments have seen their values erode with the stock market tumble. Others worked for smaller companies, or were self-employed, and never had pensions. Many are outliving whatever savings they might have had, especially by the time they reach their mid to late 70s. Mortgages and medical bills push others into the job market because Social Security and Medicare, though helpful and critical, aren't enough.

There are few programs to help older unemployed workers. Several states are developing pilot programs. The [Barack] Obama administration is receiving proposals for new ways to connect workers 55 years and older with local jobs.

"We're seeing a tremendous increase in the number of people coming for help," says Cynthia Metzler, who heads Experience Works. The Arlington, Va.-based national nonprofit organization offers job training and placement for 20,000 older adults in 30 states, and has a waiting list. The Cleveland office of another nonprofit group, the Senior Employment Center, has been seeing about 570 people coming in for help each month.

Even when the economy is humming along, older workers who get laid off tend to spend more time unemployed. In December, the average period for joblessness for workers older than 55 was 25 weeks, compared with 18.7 weeks for those under 55, according to the AARP Public Policy Institute. The physical limitations of some older workers likely account for part of the difference. But Marcie Pitt-Catsouphes, director of the Sloan Center on Aging & Work at Boston College, cites lingering stereotypes that older workers are more expensive, less productive and resistant to change.

Many [people] are outliving whatever savings they might have had, especially by the time they reach their mid to late 70s.

Today's sputtering economy has flooded the labor market with a multitude of younger workers looking for jobs, which has made it even harder for older ones.

Mr. Dase, the unemployed bartender, knows. He spent 40 years working at Pittsburgh taverns and at his own bar, never receiving a pension. Over the years, when the $1,625 Social Security check he and his wife receive each month didn't cover prescriptions or other medical costs such as supplemental Medicare insurance, they used their charge cards. Last year, when their credit card debt reached $29,000, they took out a $26,000 home equity loan to pay off most of it. He still owes $5,000 on one credit card, and needs to come up with $363 a month for eight years to pay off the home equity loan.

Mr. Dase had been working at a local Veterans of Foreign Wars club as a bartender. But he had to leave in August because it required too much standing. He looked for other jobs, applying at Big Lots stores, but he never heard back. "Who is going to hire an 81-year-old man?" he asks.

Jobs-Training Program

Three weeks ago, he entered a jobs-training program called the Senior Community Service Employment Program. The program pays him $7.15 an hour to stuff envelopes and greet visitors at the human-services center in Turtle Creek, Pa. "It helps quite a bit," he says. "Towards the end of the month, we start to run out of food. But luckily my daughter comes and helps us out."

At the moment, the Senior Community Service Program, which currently has $433 million in funding, is the lone federal jobs initiative that targets unemployed older workers. Workers must be at least 55 and not have incomes more than 25% over the poverty level—$13,000 a year for individuals. The program matches older adults with community nonprofit or public organizations. They receive on-the-job training, and are paid minimum wage, by the federal government, for up to 20 hours a week. Although it handles about 92,000 workers a year, the program is currently funded to serve less than 1% of the workers who would qualify, according to the Sloan Center, citing a Government Accountability Office [an investigative arm of Congress that tracks spending] report.

The goal is to help both unemployed older adults and community organizations, which often are short on staff. But it isn't meant to provide permanent employment. The paid training is supposed to last for no more than 24 to 36 months. Increasingly, those limits are being exceeded because there are fewer paying jobs available, especially in smaller towns and rural areas.

Lois Humphrey, 80, has trouble climbing stairs and suffers severe hearing loss, so she needs an amplifier on her phone. She had to leave her department store job because it was too hard on her feet. But she must keep working to pay for rent and prescriptions. She started at Experience Works in 2000. She has moved from one community organization to another in her Mechanicsburg, Pa., community, receiving different training along the way.

She is now back with Experience Works, the nonprofit training and placement organization, which thus far has been unable to find her a private sector job. "I've been stuck in here," she says, but gladly so. "I still need to work because of medications," says Ms. Humphrey, who has cancer, diabetes and arthritis.

Justyn Jaymes of the Senior Employment Center in Akron, which administers the federal training program locally, is expected to move 27 to 32 people a year into private sector paying jobs. They aren't supposed to spend more than 27 months in the program, on average. Several people are at that level or have exceeded it.

Older workers who get laid off tend to spend more time unemployed [in part because of] lingering stereotypes that older workers are more expensive, less productive and resistant to change.

"I'm going to have to be aggressive pushing people out in the next year," says Mr. Jaymes. He says he's always on the lookout for jobs, noticing a help wanted sign in an OfficeMax store, and whether hotels need housekeepers, janitors and breakfast hostesses.

Every week, he meets with at least four new older unemployed adults. He says he is "pretty blunt with them," telling them up front: "This is not a job. It looks like a job and feels like a job, but it is training and temporary. Are you going to job hunt or get comfortable?" Those accepted into the program must keep a log, recording their job-hunting efforts.

Getting hired isn't impossible. Dorothy Adams, 90, who raised six sons, had been a waitress. She quit at age 85 because of the physical demands. She couldn't make it on $8,000 a year in Social Security and $1,140 in food stamps, so she enrolled in an Experience Works training program in central Pennsylvania.

She got a job last year at a home health care agency. She drives to the homes of elderly adults who are sick and homebound. She reads them their mail, takes them to appointments, helps them dress and prepares light meals. She gets paid $7.50 an hour, plus mileage reimbursement.

Ms. Bennett, the laid-off machinist, had worked steadily since she entered a dress factory at the age of 17, taking time off only for the births of her seven children and a quintuple-bypass surgery in 1995. After a divorce, she worked two jobs, assembling coffee pots in the day and working at truck stops or tending bar at night. When one factory or shop or restaurant closed, she would look for another with a help wanted sign posted in the window.

In her mid 70s, she left the truck stop hoping to retire, but found that she couldn't afford to. She applied at a machine shop in central Pennsylvania. Although she had never been a machinist, she got the job, and began making parts for door hinges, trucks, cranes and guns for $9 an hour. "I'm an easy person to teach," she says.

Laid Off

Ms. Bennett and a few dozen others were laid off last March. She applied at restaurants, stores and the local mall, which needed a cleaning person. She had two interviews. They seemed to go well, but she never heard back. "I thought I had a good chance, but a lot of places want to hire younger people," she says.

As weeks passed, with no luck, she applied for unemployment for the first time in her life. She continued hunting for work before resorting to the federal job-training program.

About a month ago, she started at the cafeteria of a local hospital, waiting on customers and running the cash register for $7.15 an hour. She works five hours a day, four days a week.

Her children, including her oldest, who is retired, want her to retire. "I don't have the money to do that," Ms. Bennett says. "I couldn't plan for retirement because I was raising seven children, and it just took all the money."

Ms. Appleby, of Akron, is still without a job. For 18 years, she had worked at a small snack shop in the basement of the Summit County Courthouse. She cooked, cleaned tables and served. As her knees got weak and she relied increasingly on a cane, she was stationed at the cash register.

She earned only minimum wage, but it helped supplement her $723-a-month Social Security check, and was enough to make her house payments. Five years ago, she tore down her childhood home, which needed too many costly repairs, and built a small white bungalow in its place. Ms. Appleby, who never married and has outlived most of her relatives, other than a few far-flung cousins, took out a loan—a move she now regrets.

Last year, sales at the snack shop, called Buddy's Place, fell as more office workers began packing lunches and governments trimmed staff, resulting in fewer people stopping for coffee and soup. The owner, Aaron Hopkins, who is 36 and blind, watched labor costs balloon to 29% of sales. That put him in danger of losing his own business. Under a state program for the visually impaired that got him the snack shop job, he had to keep labor costs down to no more than 20% of sales. Mr. Hopkins, who earned $22,000 last year, reluctantly laid off Ms. Appleby.

Her mobility and age limit her options. She doesn't have a résumé. A local law firm organized a benefit to help her get through the winter and pay mortgage bills. "It is our way, as courthouse family, to try to do something to help her get back on her feet," says Jonathan Sinn, an Akron attorney. Given her age and health, Mr. Sinn doubts she will be able to get another job in the courthouse.

She is considering knee surgery, which may make her more mobile, and thus more marketable. She is applying for unemployment.

"I was waiting to see if [Mr. Hopkins] would call me back, and he hasn't," says Ms. Appleby. She lives modestly, with Timmy, a 13-year-old white spaniel mix, amid piles of papers, boxes and a lone black-and-white photo from her high school graduation. "I was fine with Social Security and my job. I have to find other work."

The Elderly Are Vulnerable to Fraud and Financial Abuse

Investor Protection Trust

The Investor Protection Trust is a nonprofit organization that provides independent, objective information needed by consumers to make informed investment decisions. To find more about this organization please visit www.investorprotection.org.

More than 7.3 million older Americans—one out of every five citizens over the age of 65—already have been victimized by a financial swindle, according to a major new Investor Protection Trust (IPT) survey conducted by Infogroup/ORC [Opinion Research Corporation] and released today [June 15, 2010] to mark World Elder Abuse Awareness Day.

The survey results underscore the urgent need for a new partnership between the nonprofit Investor Protection Trust, the North American Securities Administrators Association (NASAA), and the National Adult Protective Services Association (NAPSA) in cooperation with leading U.S. medical associations including the American Academy of Family Physicians, the National Area Health Education Center Organization, and the National Association of Geriatric Education Centers. The "Elder Investment Fraud and Financial Exploitation" prevention campaign will educate medical professionals about how to spot older Americans who may be particularly vulnerable to financial abuse and then to refer suspected investment fraud involving these at-risk patients to state securities regulators and/or to local Adult Protective Services (APS) professionals. . . .

Investor Protection Trust, "Survey: 1 Out of 5 Older Americans Are Financial Swindle Victims," June 15, 2010. www.investorprotection.org Copyright © 2010 by Investor Protection Trust. Reproduced by permission.

Key Survey Findings

Key findings of the IPT survey of 2,022 American adults—
including 706 adult children with at least one parent aged 65
or older and 590 adults who are aged 65 or older and have
children—include the following:

- Half of older Americans exhibit one or more of the
  warning signs of current financial victimization. For
  example, more than one out of three seniors (37
  percent) are currently being pitched by "people (who)
  are calling me or mailing me asking for money, lotter-
  ies, and other schemes," while a much lower 19 percent
  of adult children believe that their parents are being
  pressured in such a fashion.

- Almost half of those aged 65 or over (44 percent) got
  at least two out of four questions wrong about basic
  investment knowledge.

- About one out of three older Americans (31 percent)
  says they are vulnerable in one or more ways to potential financial victimization.

- Only 5 percent of adult children in touch with their
  parents' doctors report "the health care providers ever
  mention[ing] any concerns about your parents handling of money or relayed any concern from your parent about handling money." However, of that same
  group, nearly one in five (19 percent) reports the health
  care provider has mentioned concerns about "your
  parents' mental comprehension." Only 2 percent of
  Americans aged 65 or older say that their health care
  provider has ever asked about "how you are handling
  money issues or problems."

- Four out of 10 children of parents 65 or older are
  "very" or "somewhat" worried that their parents "have

already become or will become less able to handle their personal finances over time." Among those over the age of 65, more than a third (36 percent) are "very" or "somewhat" worried about being less able to handle money issues over time.

IPT President and CEO Don Blandin said: "We now know that a shockingly large number of older Americans are already victims of financial swindles and millions more are in danger of being exploited in such a fashion. Given that frontline medical professionals who deal everyday with older Americans are ideally positioned to spot the impaired mental capacity that can leave seniors vulnerable to financial abuse, our new program seeks to inform doctors, nurses and others about the warning signs of elder investment fraud and financial exploitation. Our goal is to improve the communication among medical professionals, older Americans, adult children and state securities regulators in order to head off financial swindles before the damage is done." . . .

The "Elder Investment Fraud and Financial Exploitation" prevention campaign will educate medical professionals about how to spot older Americans who may be particularly vulnerable to financial abuse.

NAPSA Executive Director Kathleen Quinn said: "The National Adult Protective Services Association represents the 'boots on the ground' in the fight against elder abuse. Adult Protective Services professionals are the first responders to elder financial abuse, so they see the devastation these crimes wreak in older persons' lives every day. It is imperative that a serious national campaign be launched to end rampant elder financial exploitation and to protect and help vulnerable older victims."

About the New Program

The "Elder Investment Fraud and Financial Exploitation" project will allow collaborators to work as a team to refer cases to each other, whether it is to report fraud to securities regulators, report abuse to Adult Protective Services (APS) workers, or refer a patient to a clinician for further medical evaluation.

Of particular concern are seniors with mild cognitive impairment who can perform most daily functions, but have trouble or become confused with others, like following their medicine regimen and managing their finances. A 2008 Duke University study found that about 35 percent of the 25 million people over age 71 in the U.S. either have mild cognitive impairment or Alzheimer's disease. This makes them especially vulnerable to financial exploitation, including investment fraud. . . .

More Results of the Survey

- More than three out of 10 older Americans (31 percent) say they are vulnerable in one or more ways to potential financial victimization. . . .

- 71 percent of those over 65 handle finances themselves, 24 percent rely on relatives for at least some help and 3 percent rely on nonfamily members, according to their children.

- 89 percent of children are "very confident" or "somewhat confident" of their parents' *current* ability to handle personal finances. Only 11 percent are "not very confident" or "not confident" at all. This contrasts with the views of those aged 65 or older: 97 percent say they are "very" or "somewhat" confident about their *current* ability to handle money and just 3 percent who are "not very confident" or "not confident at all" with handling personal finances.

- 80 percent of children think that their parents aged 65 or older would tell them "immediately" if they were swindled, compared to 16 percent who think their parents would be ashamed and hide such a fact. Separately, over a third (35 percent) of children say it is not likely or not very likely at all that they would be able to figure out that their parents had been swindled if their parents did not disclose that fact.

The Elderly in Nursing Homes Are Vulnerable to Abuse

David Couch

David Couch is a lawyer in Little Rock, Arkansas.

We think of nursing homes as safe havens, places where people go when they can no longer be cared for at home. Federal law—and common decency—demands that these homes provide their residents with a comfortable and dignified existence. While many facilities do live up to this nurturing ideal, too many others have failed.

In lawsuits and newspaper articles, stories about ill-treatment and shoddy medical care at nursing homes are making regular appearances. How did this sad situation come about?

To its residents, a nursing home is home; but to the owner, it is a business. These two propositions do not necessarily have to conflict with each other, but many owners have put their desire for profits over the residents' needs, and the result is unnecessary suffering.

Most of today's nursing homes are operated by for-profit companies owned by large corporate chains. According to the American Health Care Association, in December 2007, there were 15,772 certified nursing homes in the United States, housing 1.4 million residents. June 2008 data shows that for-profit nursing homes account for 67 percent of all facilities, and 53.3 percent are owned by multi-facility organizations (chains).

This was not always the case. Before 1965, most nursing homes were mom-and-pop operations. . . .

David Couch, "Corporate Neglect in Nursing Homes: Over the Years, Government Agencies and Independent Investigators Have Found Rampant Abuse and Neglect in Nursing Homes. So Far, Nursing Home Owners Have Evaded Responsibility, but That May Be Starting to Change," *Trial*, September 2008. Reproduced by permission.

Last year [2007], Ronald Silva, president of an investment firm that recently purchased one of the larger corporate nursing home chains in the country, told the *New York Times* that "there's essentially unlimited consumer demand as the baby boomers age. . . . I've never seen a surer bet."

To its residents, a nursing home is home; but to the owner, it is a business.

Nursing Home Regulations

Congress enacted regulations for nursing homes in the late 1960s and early 1970s. These largely focused on the homes' structural capacity to provide care and not on the quality of resident care. In the mid-1970s, reports of substandard care, fraud, and abuse began to surface. In 1986, the Institute of Medicine (IOM) issued a study of nursing homes that recommended several legislative changes to ensure better care.

In 1987, many of the IOM recommendations became law. Regulations promulgated under the Omnibus Budget Reconciliation Act of 1987 (OBRA 87) stated that residents are entitled "to attain or maintain the highest practicable physical, mental, and psychosocial well-being." Any nursing home that receives Medicare or Medicaid funds must abide by the regulations, and violators are subject to sanctions.

Other provisions forbid the use of physical or chemical restraints for discipline or convenience and outlaw clinically avoidable pressure sores or contractures (loss of motion). The rules mandated nutritional standards that would maintain a resident's body weight and hydration at healthy levels and established the standard that all facilities have sufficient staff to ensure the delivery of these services.

Perpetual Problems

The laws look good on paper, but reports by many government and nonprofit organizations have indicated that serious problems still exist in nursing homes. In July 2003, the Government Accountability Office (GAO) told Congress that the proportion of nursing homes with serious quality problems was "unacceptably high." And in March 2007, the GAO reported that efforts to strengthen federal enforcement of nursing home regulations had not deterred some homes from repeatedly harming residents. Exposés about nursing home abuse have become regular features in newspapers and on television.

Many of these problems are not hard to fix. The most common injuries to residents—pressure sores, contractures, malnutrition, dehydration, falls, and injuries due to medication errors—could easily be avoided it the nursing homes complied with the federal regulations and were sufficiently staffed.

In a June 2002 report to the Senate committees on aging and finance, the GAO determined that the quality of care in nursing homes is related more to staffing than to spending. "In the states we examined," the report said, "nursing hours per resident day—especially nurses' aide hours—were related to quality-of-care deficiencies, with homes providing more nursing hours being less likely to have identified quality problems than homes providing fewer nursing hours."

Researchers at the University of California, San Francisco, analyzed nursing home staffing from 1999 through 2005 and found that the average number of hours per resident day for registered nurses had declined from 0.8 in 1999 to 0.6 in 2005, while the average number of hours per resident day for licensed practical nurses remained constant at 0.7 during the same time period. The average number of nursing aide hours increased, from 2.1 to 2.3. In 2005, the number of nursing staff hours per resident day totaled 3.7.

That same analysis showed that the average number of deficiencies per facility increased from 5.7 in 1999 to 9.2 in 2004, but then decreased to 7.1 in 2005. The average number of nursing hours has remained essentially flat, while the quality of care has not improved—or has decreased.

Evidence points to a link between the number of staff hours and problems at nursing homes. Put simply, the higher the number of staff hours, the better the care, and the lower the number of staff hours, the worse the care.

In testimony before the Senate Special Committee on Aging in 2002, the GAO said the number of nursing "homes cited for deficiencies involving actual harm to residents or placing them at risk of death or serious injury remained unacceptably high." In another report to Congress that same year, the GAO said more could be done to protect residents from abuse, specifically physical and sexual abuse.

Put simply, the higher the number of staff hours, the better the care, the lower the number of staff hours, the worse the care.

The Office of Inspector General of the U.S. Department of Health and Human Services found that in 2001, 89 percent of nursing homes were cited for at least one deficiency, an increase of 8 percent from 1998. Even more alarming, the proportion of nursing homes that received a deficiency citation in any of the three "quality of care" categories increased from 70 percent in 1998 to 78 percent in 2001.

The Staffing Problem

The obvious question is: Why don't nursing homes just hire more staff and provide better care? It seems a simple solution. The answer is simple, too: profits. The two largest items in a nursing home's budget are its number of residents (or census) on the revenue side and nurse and nurse aide staffing on the expense side. Since staffing is the easiest expense to control, a nursing home owner can make money quickly and easily by reducing the size or hours of its nursing staff. A dollar not spent or budgeted for staffing falls directly to the bottom line.

A facility that does not have adequate staff can refuse to admit more residents or discharge some of its residents. The law requires that facilities accept or keep residents only when they can provide for their needs. But nursing homes are reluctant to do this because they would give up the revenue that the residents bring in. So the result is that the homes continue to take in more residents without hiring more staff.

The nursing home industry claims it is not making enough money to beef up its staff. In 2006, the Centers for Medicare & Medicaid Services (CMS) estimated that $124.9 billion was spent on nursing home care. Of this, $78.1 billion was paid by the federal government and $46.8 billion by private funds.

In comparison, in 1970, CMS estimated that the money spent on nursing home care totaled only $4 billion. Surely an increase of more than $120 billion should be adequate for the industry to provide care that meets government standards and also to make a reasonable profit.

In 2002, *U.S. News & World Report* conducted an investigation of nursing homes' claims that their expenses outstripped their profits. The magazine found that many nursing homes had healthy profit margins—often 20 percent to 30 percent—and that substantial portions of their revenues were diverted into subsidiary or related companies. As much as $3.4 billion went into these so-called related-party transactions, which typically involve exporting profits to a nursing home's parent company, allocating some of the parent company's costs to the nursing home, and purchasing goods and services from related parties. *U.S. News & World Report* determined that this self-dealing was widespread, with 7 out of 10 homes engaged in such practices.

The investigation also uncovered the fact that much of the money pumped into nursing homes by the federal government had not been spent on staffing increases. . . .

Recently, the *New York Times* examined data collected by government agencies from 2000 to 2006 and concluded that some nursing homes that were acquired by large private investors had cut staff and other expenses to levels below the legal minimum requirements. And many of these homes scored worse than the national averages in 12 of 14 indicators that regulators use to track ailments of nursing home residents.

In the past, the liability of these parent corporations or individual decision makers was predicated on the legal theory of piercing the corporate veil. While this theory may still work in some instances, corporate defense attorneys have developed solid strategies to defeat it, so your best approach is to pursue alternative liability theories.

The strongest cause of action in these circumstances is an action for direct liability against a parent corporation and its executive decision makers. Executives who know that residents are being neglected—know that adequate resources, including staff, are not being provided—and reward administrators for increasing profits instead of providing good care can and must be held responsible.

Executives who know that residents are being neglected— know that adequate resources, including staff, are not being provided—and reward administrators for increasing profits instead of providing good care can and must be held responsible.

One recent case that illustrates this principle of direct liability well, although it is not a nursing home case, is *Forsythe v. Clark USA, Inc.* A parent company, an oil refiner, instructed one of its subsidiaries to use a budget strategy that required the subsidiary to cut operating costs for training, maintenance, supervision, and safety. As a direct result, unqualified and untrained employees caused a fire that killed two people.

The Illinois Supreme Court held that "a parent corporation can be held liable if, for its own benefit, it directs or authorizes the manner in which its subsidiary's budget is implemented, disregarding the discretion and interests of the subsidiary, and thereby creating, dangerous conditions."

In nursing homes, the link between staffing and quality of care is clear. If cuts in staff and resources in a nursing home lead to harm, then whoever made the decision to make those cuts should be held accountable to those harmed by it.

Some Elders Must Take Drastic Measures to Obtain Long-Term Care

Mary A. Fischer

Mary A. Fischer is a journalist who has written for many national magazines.

In 2004 Roberta H. and her husband, Alex, both 64, were living a contented life in a small town in western Massachusetts. Married for 39 years, with two grown sons, they had saved for years and were looking forward to traveling in a year or so, once they retired from their respective jobs—Alex was a college English professor, and Roberta was director of communications for a consortium of local colleges.

Then disaster struck. Alex was diagnosed with early-stage dementia and took early retirement from his job. Determined to care for her husband at home, Roberta paid various people—at a cost of about $1,000 a month—to take him for walks, drive him to the Y [community center], and prepare his lunch. She filled in the gaps by phoning him several times a day.

As his dementia worsened, though, Alex needed full-time care, so Roberta found an adult-daycare center that could care for him while she worked. For 18 months Roberta dropped off Alex in the mornings and picked him up after work, a routine that went well until he had a medical emergency and landed in the hospital. Medicare paid for Alex's stay, but after three days the hospital released him, even though he could barely walk. "It was such a stressful time," says Roberta. "I had no time to figure out where Alex should go to get the therapy he needed."

After a flurry of phone calls, she found a skilled nursing home that didn't have a waiting list, but there was a big catch: Medicare would cover only a total of 100 days of skilled care and rehab. When the coverage ended, Roberta began drawing on the couple's savings, paying the nursing home $7,500 a month, plus miscellaneous expenses. Eight months and $75,000 later, the stock market crashed and cut the couple's savings in half.

"I was so scared," Roberta recalls. "Not only was my husband disappearing, but our savings were, too. All I could think was, if something happened to me, there'd be nothing left and I'd be out on the street." At the urging of a financial counselor, she made an appointment with a respected elder-law attorney. When he laid out her options, only one—divorce—allowed her to get care for her husband and hang on to their remaining savings. By divorcing Alex, the love of her life, Roberta would render him indigent, thus eligible for Medicaid.

"I felt terribly depressed and guilty," says Roberta, "but I felt I had no choice." She received the final divorce papers on August 15, 2008, the day before the couple's 44th wedding anniversary.

Spending down assets to qualify for Medicaid often means that the healthy spouse is left with insufficient assets for his or her own retirement.

Too Few Options

Roberta and Alex are not alone. Like many older Americans, they find they must make gut-wrenching choices—to divorce a spouse, or to file papers refusing to pay for an institutionalized spouse, a practice known as "spousal refusal."

The two existing national health insurance programs—Medicare and Medicaid—have, in part, created the conditions that have led people to take these drastic measures. Medicare, the health insurance program for those 65 and over, was designed largely to treat acute medical conditions and does not pay for more than 100 days of skilled nursing care and rehab therapy.

Medicaid, the health insurance program for the poor, does pay for nursing home care, but only after an individual has "spent down" his or her assets—that is, he or she has depleted all cash assets, including stocks, except for a nominal amount, usually $2,000. Spending down assets by transferring them to children is not a viable option because Medicaid looks for gifts the person made within the five years prior to applying for Medicaid and then denies coverage for the number of months the gift could have paid for nursing home care.

The viable options can be bleak, however. If the person is married, spending down assets to qualify for Medicaid often means that the healthy spouse is left with insufficient assets for his or her retirement. (The "community spouse"—the spouse who doesn't need nursing home care—can keep the couple's home but just half their savings.) "Requiring people who have worked hard and saved all their lives to become impoverished before they qualify for long-term care through Medicaid is draconian, demeaning, and disempowering," says James Firman, president and CEO of the National Council on Aging. "It is also terrible social policy and can't be sustained."

A look at the numbers reveals just how precarious the system is. Americans who live to 65 have a 40 percent chance of entering a nursing home during their lifetime. The average stay lasts 2.5 years and costs about $175,000. In 2008, the most recent year for which numbers are available, 9 million people 65 and older needed long-term care. That number is expected to reach 12 million by 2020 as the boomer population ages. Currently, only about 8 million Americans have private long-term care insurance.

Critics of asset transfers point to the staggering costs of Medicaid—$333.2 billion in 2007—and maintain that those who dodge their responsibility to pay for their own long-term care are gaming the system. But elder advocates say these practices go on because Medicare and Medicaid haven't done enough to support home- and community-based services. Medicaid, in particular, is overly focused on nursing home care, with far fewer resources allotted for home care. "Powerful state nursing home lobbies make it very difficult to break the institutional bias in Medicaid," says Firman. "Medicaid spends 75 percent of its long-term funding on putting people in costly nursing homes rather than finding ways to keep people in their own homes and communities."

Forced into a Nursing Home

Donna T., 41, vividly remembers the day in 2008 when she broke the sad news to her father that his family could no longer afford to care for him in his home. Already partially disabled at 63 by a stroke, Donna's dad had suffered a painful obstructed bowel, which landed him in the hospital for ten days. The rock of their family, he had retired early so he could take care of his diabetic wife and his mother, who had dementia. But now, barely able to walk, he couldn't take care of himself, let alone them.

Donna had hoped her father could recover at home, but the financial obstacles proved overwhelming. At 64 he was still a year away from qualifying for Medicare, and his private health insurance didn't cover long-term rehabilitative care. Neither Donna nor her siblings could afford skilled nursing care, and the $7,000 a month for a nursing home would wipe out her parents' savings in nine months. The vexing question became: How do we care for Dad without putting Mom out on the street?

Medicaid was the only answer. Summoning up her courage, Donna informed her father that he had to spend down his half of her parents' assets to meet the Medicaid asset poverty level of $2,000. "I've done everything right in my life," he told his daughter, "and now I have to be poor?"

There was more. In order for him to get the rehab therapy he needed, Medicaid required that he move into a nursing home. Six months later, he died. "It broke my heart," says Donna. "My father died in that nursing home thinking he had nothing. He hated living there. But it was the best we could do, given the financial circumstances."

Advocates for the elderly have long argued that Medicare and Medicaid should devote more resources to keeping people in their homes and communities as long as possible. Likewise, AARP [an advocacy organization for older Americans] research shows that nine out of ten Americans prefer to remain in their homes as they age. And though funding for home- and community-based services has increased (from $17 billion to $38 billion) from 1999 to 2006, according to the Kaiser Commission on Medicaid and the Uninsured, those dollars are dwarfed by the $60 billion Medicaid spent on institutionalized care in 2006.

Advocates for the elderly have long argued that Medicare and Medicaid should devote more resources to keeping people in their homes and communities as long as possible.

Proposed Solutions

Some advocates see Medicaid's complicated spend-down policies (which vary from state to state) as part of the problem and want to get Medicaid out of the long-term care business. "The disadvantage of Medicaid's funding long-term care is that it is a poverty program that has limited public access and fragmented services," says Steven P. Wallace, PhD, associate director of UCLA's [University of California, Los Angeles's] Center for Health Policy Research. Others have proposed that

Medicare provide long-term care as a benefit, in much the same way it provides the Part D drug [prescription drug coverage] benefit today. Still others want a national long-term care insurance program, something like the CLASS [Community Living Assistance Services and Supports] Act proposed by the late senator Edward Kennedy.[1]

Meanwhile, back in Massachusetts, Roberta still wrestles with her agonizing decision to divorce her husband so he could qualify for Medicaid. She has found some peace in the realization that "marriage means more than a piece of paper." Her love and devotion to Alex have not diminished, and she visits him every day in the nursing home, giving him the latest news about their children. Totally incapacitated now, both physically and mentally, Alex will never improve or return home. But Roberta is grateful for the time they have as well as the peace of mind that comes with knowing her own future is secure. "I'm grateful I still have my home and enough savings so I won't be dependent on my children," she says. "But the real question is, why should health care have to end up in the courts? What kind of a system is that?"

---

1. The CLASS Act was signed into law on March 23, 2010, as part of the Patient Protection and Affordable Care Act. It covers the creation of a disability insurance program.

Organizations to Contact

The editors have compiled the following list of organizations concerned with the issues debated in this book. The descriptions are derived from materials provided by the organizations. All have publications or information available for interested readers. The list was compiled on the date of publication of the present volume; the information provided here may change. Be aware that many organizations take several weeks or longer to respond to inquiries, so allow as much time as possible.

AARP
601 E Street NW, Washington, DC   20049
(888) 687-2277
website: www.aarp.org

AARP, the nation's largest membership organization for people fifty years of age and older, is a nonprofit, nonpartisan organization that advocates legislation to benefit older Americans and aims to help them improve the quality of their lives. It publishes *AARP: The Magazine*, the largest-circulation magazine in the world, as well as the *AARP Bulletin*. Its website contains extensive information on many topics of interest to older adults.

Administration on Aging (AoA)
Washington, DC   20201
(202) 619-0724 • fax: (202) 357-3555
e-mail: aoainfo@aoa.hhs.gov
website: www.aoa.gov

The Administration on Aging (AoA) is a part of the U.S. Department of Health and Human Services. Its mission is to develop a comprehensive, coordinated, and cost-effective system of home and community-based services that helps elderly individuals maintain their health and independence in their homes and communities. Its website features information about its programs and detailed statistics about aging Americans.

Alliance for Retired Americans

815 Sixteenth Street NW, Fourth Floor
Washington, DC 20006
(202) 637-5399
website: www.retiredamericans.org

The Alliance for Retired Americans is a nonprofit, nonpartisan organization of retired trade union members. Its mission is to ensure social and economic justice and full civil rights for all citizens so that they may enjoy lives of dignity, personal and family fulfillment, and security. Its website contains information about legislative issues affecting retired persons.

American Bar Association Commission on Law and Aging

740 Fifteenth Street NW, Washington, DC 20005-1022
(202) 662-8690 • fax: (202) 662-8698
e-mail: abaaging@abanet.org
website: http://new.abanet.org/aging

The mission of the American Bar Association Commission on Law and Aging is to strengthen and secure the legal rights, dignity, autonomy, quality of life, and quality of care of elders. It carries out this mission through research, policy development, technical assistance, advocacy, education, and training. Its website contains information about legal issues affecting elders, such as housing needs, public benefit programs, guardianship, elder abuse, health care decision making, and end-of-life care.

Gray Panthers

1612 K Street NW, Suite 300, Washington, DC 20006
(800) 280-5362 • fax: (202) 737-1160
e-mail: info@graypanthers.org
website: http://graypanthers.org

The Gray Panthers is an intergenerational, multi-issue organization seeking intergenerational approaches to achieving social and economic justice and peace. Its values include honoring maturity, unifying generations, and actively engaging in social and political causes. Its website contains news and information about issues with which it is concerned and a "soap box" blog.

National Association of Area Agencies on Aging (N4A)

1730 Rhode Island Avenue NW, Suite 1200
Washington, DC 20036
(202) 872-0888 • fax: (202) 872-0057
website: www.n4a.org

The primary mission of the National Association of Area Agencies on Aging (N4A) is to build the capacity of its members to help older persons and individuals with disabilities live with dignity in their homes and communities for as long as possible. Its website contains many reports and consumer publications, plus information on the National Center on Senior Transportation, which it administers.

National Center on Elder Abuse (NCEA)

c/o Center for Community Research and Services
University of Delaware, 297 Graham Hall, Newark, DE   19716
(302) 831-3525 • fax: (302) 831-4225
e-mail: ncea-info@aoa.hhs.gov
website: www.ncea.aoa.gov

The National Center on Elder Abuse (NCEA), directed by the U.S. Administration on Aging, is committed to helping national, state, and local partners in the field be fully prepared to ensure that older Americans live with dignity, integrity, and independence, and without abuse, neglect, and exploitation. It is a resource for policy makers, social service and health care practitioners, the justice system, researchers, advocates, and families. Its website contains information about elder abuse, how to prevent it, and resources for those affected by it.

National Institute on Aging
Building 31, Room 5C27, 31 Center Drive, MSC 2292
Bethesda, MD   20892
(301) 496-1752 • fax: (301) 496-1072
website: www.nia.nih.gov

The National Institute on Aging (NIA), one of the congressionally authorized National Institutes of Health, leads a broad scientific effort to understand the nature of aging and to extend the healthy, active years of life. Its mission is to support and conduct genetic, biological, clinical, behavioral, social, and economic research related to aging and to communicate information about aging and advances in research to the scientific community, health care providers, and the public. Its website contains such information, with links to external resources including a list of more than three hundred organizations that provide help to older people.

Bibliography

Books

Daniel Callahan — *Taming the Beloved Beast: How Medical Technology Costs Are Destroying Our Health Care System.* Princeton, NJ: Princeton University Press, 2009.

Laura Hurd Clarke — *Facing Age: Women Growing Older in an Anti-Aging Culture.* Lanham, MD: Rowman & Littlefield, 2010.

Gene D. Cohen — *The Mature Mind: The Positive Power of the Aging Brain.* New York: Basic Books, 2005.

Thomas R. Cole, Ruth E. Ray, and Robert Kastenbaum, eds. — *A Guide to Humanistic Studies in Aging: What Does It Mean to Grow Old?* Baltimore, MD: Johns Hopkins University Press, 2010.

Ingrid Arnet Connidis — *Family Ties & Aging.* 2nd ed. Los Angeles, CA: Pine Forge Press, 2010.

Louis Cozolino — *The Healthy Aging Brain: Sustaining Attachment, Attaining Wisdom.* New York: W.W. Norton & Co., 2008.

Margaret Cruikshank — *Learning to Be Old: Gender, Culture, and Aging.* 2nd ed. Lanham, MD: Rowman & Littlefield, 2009.

Muriel R. Gillick   *The Denial of Aging: Perpetual Youth, Eternal Life, and Other Dangerous Fantasies.* Cambridge, MA: Harvard University Press, 2006.

Diana K. Harris   *The Sociology of Aging.* 3rd ed. Lanham, MD: Rowman & Littlefield, 2007.

Robert D. Hill   *Seven Strategies for Positive Aging.* New York: W.W. Norton & Co., 2008.

Robert Levine   *Aging with Attitude: Growing Older with Dignity and Vitality.* Westport, CT: Praeger, 2004.

Stephanie Marohn, ed.   *Audacious Aging.* Santa Rosa, CA: Elite Books, 2009.

Harry R. Moody   *Aging: Concepts and Controversies.* 6th ed. Los Angeles, CA: Pine Forge Press, 2010.

James H. Schulz and Robert H. Binstock   *Aging Nation: The Economics and Politics of Growing Older in America.* Baltimore, MD: Johns Hopkins University Press, 2008.

Albert J. Seme   *Elderly Abuse Is Alive and Well.* Pittsburgh, PA: Dorrance Publishing, 2009.

Neil Shulman, Michael A. Silverman, and Adam G. Golden   *The Real Truth About Aging: A Survival Guide for Older Adults and Caregivers.* Amherst, NY: Prometheus Books, 2009.

John Sloan   *A Bitter Pill: How the Medical System Is Failing the Elderly*. Vancouver, BC: Greystone Books, 2009.

Paula Span   *When the Time Comes: Families with Aging Parents Share Their Struggles and Solutions*. New York: Springboard Press, 2009.

Olga Brom Spencer   *New Frontiers in Aging: Spirit and Science to Maximize Peak Experience in Your 60s, 70s, and Beyond*. Westport, CT: Praeger, 2008.

Philip B. Stafford   *Elderburbia: Aging with a Sense of Place in America*. Santa Barbara, CA; Praeger, 2009.

Arlene Weintraub   *Selling the Fountain of Youth: How the Anti-Aging Industry Made a Disease Out of Getting Old—and Made Billions*. New York: Basic Books, 2010.

Periodicals

Marc E. Agronin   "Old Age, from Youth's Narrow Prism," *New York Times*, March 1, 2010.

Patricia Ahern   "End of Life—Not End of Story: With the Number of Seniors Rising, Hospice Care Needs Greater Attention," *Modern Healthcare*, June 18, 2007.

Nicholas Bakalar	"Happiness May Come with Age, Study Says," *New York Times*, May 31, 2010.
Jane E. Brody	"End-of-Life Issues Need to Be Addressed," *New York Times*, August 17, 2009.
Patricia Leigh Brown	"Invisible Immigrants, Old and Left with 'Nobody to Talk To,'" *New York Times*, August 30, 2009.
Stephanie Clifford	"Online, 'a Reason to Keep on Going,'" *New York Times*, June 1, 2009.
Alice Dembner	"Ageism Said to Erode Care Given to Elders," *Boston Globe*, March 7, 2005.
Claudia Dreifus	"Focusing on the Issue of Aging, and Growing into the Job," *New York Times*, November 14, 2006.
John Eligon and Benjamin Weiser	"Weighing Prison When the Convict Is over 80," *New York Times*, October 9, 2009.
Daniel Engber	"Naughty Nursing Homes," *Slate*, September 27, 2007.
Henry Fountain	"Old and Overscheduled; No, You Can't Just Dodder," *New York Times*, May 15, 2005.
Atul Gawande	"The Way We Age Now," *New Yorker*, April 30, 2007.
Steven Greenhouse	"65 and Up and Looking for Work," *New York Times*, October 23, 2009.

Jane Gross   "Faced with Caregiving, Even the Experts Struggle," *New York Times*, July 14, 2008.

Jane Gross   "Forensic Skills Seek to Uncover Elder Abuse," *New York Times*, September 27, 2006.

Rob Gurwitt   "Staying Connected," *AARP Bulletin*, March 2010.

Gaby Hinsliff   "Stop the Boomer-Bashing," *New Statesman*, January 29, 2010.

Scott James   "An Unlikely Plaintiff. At Issue? He Dares Not Speak Its Name," *New York Times*, May 7, 2010.

Kirk Johnson   "Seeing Old Age as a Never-Ending Adventure," *New York Times*, January 7, 2010.

Gina Kolata   "The Elderly Always Sleep Worse, and Other Myths of Aging," *New York Times*, October 23, 2007.

John Leland   "Sensors Help Keep the Elderly Safe, and at Home," *New York Times*, February 12, 2009.

Calum MacLeod   "A Glimpse of the Future: Robots Aid Japan's Elderly Residents," *USA Today*, November 5, 2009.

Bob Morris   "Stop Spending My Inheritance," *New York Times*, July 30, 2006.

Tara Parker-Pope   "An Epidemic of Crashes Among the Aging? Unlikely, Study Says," *New York Times*, January 12, 2009.

James Ridgeway   "The Graying of American Prisons," Crime Report, December 7, 2009. http://thecrimereport.org.

Selena Roberts   "Special Senior Moments," *Sports Illustrated*, December 28, 2009.

Peter Singer   "Why We Must Ration Health Care," *New York Times*, July 15, 2009.

Hilary Stout   "Technologies Help Adult Children Monitor Aging Parents," *New York Times*, July 28, 2010.

Stefan Theil   "The New Old Age: As the Pool of Young Recruits Dries Up, Companies and Countries Are Putting the Retired Back to Work," *Newsweek International*, January 30, 2006.

Kate Zernike   "Turn 70. Act Your Grandchild's Age," *New York Times*, July 10, 2010.

Katie Zezima   "Experiencing Life, Briefly, Inside a Nursing Home," *New York Times*, August 23, 2009.

Index